GDScript for Game Developers

A Practical Introduction

Jim P. Snell

Table of Contents

Part 1: Getting Started with GDScript

Chapter 1

Introduction to GDScript and Godot

Welcome to the exciting world of game development with GDScript and Godot! This chapter serves as your launchpad, exploring what GDScript is, why it's a fantastic choice for game development, and getting you set up with the Godot Engine. We'll even write our first GDScript program – the classic "Hello, World!" – but with some added depth.

1.1 What is GDScript and Why Use It?

GDScript is Godot's built-in scripting language, specifically designed for game development.[1] This means it's optimized for tasks like controlling game objects, handling user input, and managing game logic.

Think of it this way: Godot is the stage, and GDScript is the script that directs the actors (your game objects).

Here's why GDScript is a great choice:

- **Easy to Learn:** GDScript's syntax is similar to Python, making it relatively easy to pick up, especially if you have some prior programming experience. Even if you're a complete beginner, don't worry – we'll guide you through it.
- **Tightly Integrated with Godot:** GDScript is deeply integrated with the Godot Engine, allowing you to easily interact with every aspect of your game, from nodes in the scene tree to physical simulations.[2]
- **Performance:** GDScript is compiled to bytecode, which provides good performance without the complexities of lower-level

languages like C++.[3] It's fast enough for most game projects, especially for beginners.

- **Readability:** GDScript's clean syntax makes your code easier to read and understand.[4] This is crucial for maintaining your project and collaborating with others.

Personally, I found GDScript a breath of fresh air when I first started using Godot. It allowed me to focus on creating game mechanics without getting bogged down in complex syntax or memory management.

1.2 Setting up Godot Engine

Setting up Godot is incredibly straightforward. Here's a step-by-step guide:

1. **Download:** Head over to the official Godot Engine website: godotengine.org. This is the official source, so you can be sure you're getting a safe and up-to-date version.
2. **Choose Your Version:** Godot offers a few different versions:

Standard Version: This is the version we'll be using throughout this book, as it focuses on GDScript. It's the most common choice for beginners and many experienced developers.

Mono Version: This version adds support for C# scripting. C# is a powerful and popular language, but it adds some complexity to the setup and project structure. If you're already familiar with C# or have specific needs for it, you might consider this version. However, for learning GDScript, stick with the standard version.

Web Editor: Godot also offers a web editor that runs directly in your browser. While convenient for quick tests and experiments, it's not ideal for larger projects or offline development.

3. For this book, make sure you download the **standard version** appropriate for your operating system (Windows, macOS, Linux, etc.).

4. **Extract (if necessary):** Godot typically comes as a compressed archive (like a .zip or .tar.gz file). Once downloaded, you'll need to extract its contents. On Windows, you can usually right-click and select "Extract All." On macOS and Linux, you can use built-in archive utilities or command-line tools like unzip or tar.

5. **Run:** The beauty of Godot is that it doesn't require a traditional installation process. Once extracted (if necessary), you'll find a single executable file (e.g., Godot_v[version]_stable_[platform].exe on Windows). Just double-click this executable to launch Godot. There's no need to run an installer or worry about registry entries.

6. **Project Manager:** When you first open Godot, you'll be greeted by the Project Manager. This is the central hub for managing your Godot projects. Here you can:

Create New Projects: Click "New Project" to start a fresh project.

Import Existing Projects: Import projects you or others have created.

Manage Projects: Open, rename, or delete existing projects.

7. **Creating Your First Project:** To create your first project for this book, click "New Project."

Project Name: Give your project a descriptive name (e.g., "GDScriptIntro").

Project Path: Choose a location on your computer to save your project files. It's good practice to create a dedicated folder for your Godot projects.

Create Folder: If the chosen path doesn't exist, Godot will prompt you to create the folder. Click "Create Folder."

Create & Edit: Finally, click "Create & Edit" to create the project and open the Godot editor.

That's it! You've successfully set up Godot and created your first project. The Godot editor will now open, ready for you to start creating your games with GDScript.

1.3 Your First GDScript: "Hello, World!" (Enhanced)

Let's dive into creating your first GDScript program: the classic "Hello, World!" This exercise is more than just displaying text; it's about understanding how GDScript interacts with Godot's scene system and introduces key programming concepts.

Step 1: Setting up the Scene

1. **New Project:** If you haven't already, create a new Godot project as described in the previous section.
2. **Adding a Label:** In the Godot editor, you'll start with a default scene containing a root "Node2D." Right-click on this Node2D in the Scene dock (usually on the left side) and select "Add Child Node." Search for "Label" and add it. The Label node is a UI element that displays text.
3. **Positioning the Label (Optional):** You can adjust the Label's position and size in the viewport using the move and scale tools (the arrow and rectangle icons in the toolbar). This isn't essential for this example but is good practice for UI design.

Step 2: Adding the Script

1. **Attaching a Script:** With the Label node selected, go to the Inspector dock (usually on the right side). At the top of the Inspector, you'll see a small script icon with a plus sign (+). Click this to add a new script.
2. **Script Configuration:** A "Create Script" window will appear. Here, you can configure some settings for your script. For now, you can usually leave the default settings as they are (Language: GDScript, Template: Default). Click "Create." This action creates the script file and opens it in Godot's built-in script editor.

Step 3: Writing the GDScript Code

This is where we write the code that makes things happen. Here's the code we'll use:

```gdscript
GDScript

extends Label

func _ready():

    text = "Hello, World!"

    print("Hello from GDScript in the console!")

    print("My Node's Name is: " + name)
```

Let's break down this code line by line:

- extends Label: This line is crucial. It tells GDScript that this script is associated with a Label node and inherits all of its properties and functions. This is a fundamental concept in object-oriented programming called *inheritance*. Because of this line, we can directly use properties of the Label node, like text.

- func _ready():: This is a built-in function (also known as a *method*) in Godot. The _ready() function is automatically called by Godot when the node (in this case, our Label) enters the scene tree and is ready to be used. This is often where you put initialization code— code that sets up your node when the game starts.
- text = "Hello, World!": This line sets the text property of the Label node to the string "Hello, World!". This is what makes the text appear on the screen in your game. The = symbol is the *assignment operator*, which assigns the value on the right to the variable or property on the left.
- print("Hello from GDScript in the console!"): The print() function displays a message in Godot's Output console (usually at the bottom of the editor). This is extremely useful for debugging (finding and fixing errors in your code) and for checking the state of your game during development.
- print("My Node's Name is: " + name): This line demonstrates how to access a node's properties from GDScript. Every node has a name property that reflects its name in the scene tree. The + operator is used here to *concatenate* (join together) strings. This line will print the name of the Label node to the console.

Step 4: Running the Scene

1. **Save the Script:** Press Ctrl+S (or Cmd+S on macOS) to save your script. It's important to save your work regularly!
2. **Run the Scene:** Press F5 or click the "Play" button (the play icon) at the top of the Godot editor.

What You'll See:

- "Hello, World!" will appear on the screen in your game window.
- "Hello from GDScript in the console!" and "My Node's Name is: Label" (or whatever you named your Label node in the scene tree) will be printed in the Output console at the bottom of the Godot editor.

Deeper Insights and Personal Insights:

- **Node Hierarchy:** Godot's scenes are organized as a tree of nodes. Scripts are attached to these nodes, and they can interact with other nodes in the tree. This hierarchical structure is a powerful way to organize complex game logic. When I first started using Godot, understanding the node tree was key to making my games more manageable.
- **The _ready() Function:** Understanding the timing of the _ready() function is essential. It ensures your code runs *after* the node is fully initialized. Trying to access properties of other nodes before they are ready can lead to errors. I've definitely run into my share of those early on!
- **String Concatenation:** While the + operator works for basic string concatenation, GDScript also offers more advanced string formatting options (which we'll cover later).

This enhanced explanation provides a more thorough understanding of the "Hello, World!" example and lays the groundwork for more advanced GDScript concepts. We've not only displayed text but also explored how GDScript interacts with the Godot Engine and touched on important programming concepts like inheritance, functions, and debugging.

Chapter 2

GDScript Basics: Variables, Data Types, and Operators

In this chapter, we'll cover the fundamental building blocks of GDScript: variables, data types, and operators. These concepts are essential for any programming language, and mastering them will allow you to write more complex and dynamic game logic.

2.1 Declaring and Using Variables

Variables are fundamental building blocks in programming. They act as containers for storing data within your program. Think of them as labeled boxes where you can put different kinds of information. In GDScript, you declare a variable using the var keyword.

Here's the basic syntax:

GDScript

```
var variable_name = value
```

- var: This keyword tells GDScript you're creating a new variable.
- variable_name: This is the name you give to your variable. Choose descriptive names that clearly indicate what the variable stores. Using snake_case (lowercase words separated by underscores,

like player_score or enemy_health) is the recommended convention in GDScript.

- =: This is the assignment operator. It assigns the value on the right to the variable on the left.
- value: This is the data you want to store in the variable.

Examples:

GDScript

var player_health = 100 # Stores an integer (whole number)

var player_name = "Bob" # Stores a string (text)

var is_jumping = false # Stores a boolean (true or false)

var speed = 5.5 # Stores a float (decimal number)

Type Inference:

GDScript uses *type inference*, which means you don't always have to explicitly specify the data type of a variable. GDScript will often figure it out based on the value you assign.

- var my_number = 10 (GDScript infers my_number is an integer)
- var my_text = "Hello" (GDScript infers my_text is a string)

Explicit Type Declaration:

While type inference is convenient, you can also explicitly declare the type of a variable using a colon : after the variable name:

GDScript

```
var my_integer: int = 10

var my_float: float = 3.14

var my_string: String = "Hello"

var my_bool: bool = false
```

Explicit type declaration can improve code readability, especially in larger projects, and helps catch potential type-related errors early on. I often find that explicitly declaring types helps me keep track of what kind of data I'm working with, especially when I come back to code I haven't looked at in a while.

Using Variables:

Once you've declared a variable, you can use it throughout your script:

GDScript

```
var score = 0

score = score + 5 # Adds 5 to the score
```

```
print("Current score: " + str(score)) # Prints the current score (convert integer to
string)

var message = "Hello, "

var name = "Alice"

print(message + name) # Prints "Hello, Alice"
```

Important Considerations:

- **Variable Scope:** The *scope* of a variable determines where in your code it can be accessed. We'll cover scope in more detail later, but for now, keep in mind that variables declared within a function are generally only accessible within that function.
- **Case Sensitivity:** GDScript is case-sensitive. myVariable is different from myvariable.
- **Naming Conventions:** Stick to clear and descriptive names. This makes your code easier to understand and maintain.

This explanation provides a solid foundation for understanding how to declare and use variables in GDScript. It's a fundamental concept that you'll use constantly in your game development journey.

2.2 Common Data Types: int, float, String, bool

In GDScript, as in most programming languages, data types categorize the kind of values a variable can hold.[1] Understanding these types is crucial for writing correct and efficient code. Here's a breakdown of the common data types you'll encounter in GDScript:

- **int (Integer):** Integers represent whole numbers, both positive and negative, without any decimal points. Examples: -5, 0, 10, 12345. Integers are commonly used for counting, indexing, and representing discrete quantities.

Example in GDScript: var player_score: int = 100

- **float (Floating-Point Number):** Floats represent numbers with decimal points.[2] They are used for representing fractional values or numbers with greater precision.[3] Examples: 3.14, -2.7, 0.0, 1.23e5 (scientific notation).

Example in GDScript: var player_speed: float = 7.5

- **String:** Strings represent sequences of characters (text).[4] They are enclosed in double quotes ("). Examples: "Hello", "Game Over", "Player Name". Strings are used for displaying text, storing messages, and handling textual data.

Example in GDScript: var message: String = "Welcome to the game!"

- **bool (Boolean):** Booleans represent truth values: true or false. They are used for logical operations, conditional statements, and representing binary states (on/off, yes/no).[5]

Example in GDScript: var is_game_over: bool = false

Key Differences and Considerations:

- **Integer vs. Float:** The main difference is the presence of a decimal point.[6] If you need to represent fractional values, use a float. If you're working with whole numbers only, use an integer for better performance.

- **String Concatenation:** You can combine strings using the + operator. For example:

GDScript

var greeting: String = "Hello, "

var name: String = "Alice"

var full_greeting: String = greeting + name # full_greeting will be "Hello, Alice"

- **Type Conversion:** Sometimes, you might need to convert a value from one type to another. GDScript provides functions for this, such as str() (converts to string), int() (converts to integer), and float() (converts to float). For example:

GDScript

var score: int = 10

var score_string: String = str(score) # score_string will be "10"

Type Safety (Optional): While GDScript uses type inference, you can also explicitly declare types as shown in the examples above using the colon :. This can help catch type-related errors during development.

Understanding these basic data types is essential for working with variables and performing operations in GDScript. They form the foundation for more complex data structures and programming concepts that we'll cover later.

2.3 Arithmetic, Comparison, and Logical Operators

Operators are special symbols that perform operations on values (operands).[1] In GDScript, you'll use three main categories of operators: arithmetic, comparison, and logical. Let's break them down:

Arithmetic Operators: These operators perform mathematical calculations.[2]

- + (Addition): Adds two values. Example: 5 + 3 results in 8.
- - (Subtraction): Subtracts one value from another. Example: 10 - 4 results in 6.
- * (Multiplication): Multiplies two values. Example: 2 * 6 results in 12.
- / (Division): Divides one value by another. Example: 15 / 3 results in 5.0 (note that division results in a float).
- % (Modulo): Returns the remainder after division. Example: 10 % 3 results in 1 (because 10 divided by 3 is 3 with a remainder of 1).

Example in GDScript:

GDScript

```
var a: int = 10

var b: int = 5

var addition: int = a + b # 15
```

var subtraction: int = a - b # 5

var multiplication: int = a * b # 50

var division: float = a / b # 2.0 (Important: result is a float)

var modulo: int = a % b # 0

print("Addition: " + str(addition))

print("Subtraction: " + str(subtraction))

print("Multiplication: " + str(multiplication))

print("Division: " + str(division))

print("Modulo: " + str(modulo))

Comparison Operators: These operators compare two values and return a boolean result (true or false).

- == (Equal to): Checks if two values are[3] equal. Example: 5 == 5 results in true. 5 == 6 results in false.
- != (Not equal to): Checks if two values are not equal. Example: 5 != 3 results in true. 5 != 5 results in false.
- > (Greater than): Checks if the left value is greater than the right value. Example: 8 > 5 results in true.
- < (Less than): Checks if the left value is less than the right value. Example: 2 < 7 results in true.
- >= (Greater than or equal to): Checks if the left value is greater than or equal to the right value. Example: 5 >= 5 results in true. 6 >= 5 also results in true.

- <= (Less than or equal to): Checks if the left value is less than or equal to the right value. Example: 3 <= 6 results in true. 6 <= 6 also results in true.

Example in GDScript:

```gdscript
GDScript

var x: int = 10

var y: int = 5

var equal: bool = x == y # false

var not_equal: bool = x != y # true

var greater_than: bool = x > y # true

var less_than: bool = x < y # false

var greater_than_or_equal_to: bool = x >= y # true

var less_than_or_equal_to: bool = x <= y # false

print("Equal: " + str(equal))

print("Not Equal: " + str(not_equal))

print("Greater Than: " + str(greater_than))

print("Less Than: " + str(less_than))

print("Greater Than or Equal To: " + str(greater_than_or_equal_to))

print("Less Than or Equal To: " + str(less_than_or_equal_to))
```

Logical Operators: These operators combine or modify boolean values.

- and: Logical AND. Returns true if *both* operands are true. Otherwise, it returns false.
- or: Logical OR. Returns true if *at least one* of the operands is true. Returns false only if both are false.
- not: Logical NOT. Inverts the boolean value. If the operand is true, not returns false, and vice-versa.

Example in GDScript:

```gdscript
GDScript

var p: bool = true

var q: bool = false

var logical_and: bool = p and q # false

var logical_or: bool = p or q # true

var logical_not_p: bool = not p # false

print("Logical AND: " + str(logical_and))

print("Logical OR: " + str(logical_or))

print("Logical NOT p: " + str(logical_not_p))
```

Combining Operators: You can combine these operators to create more complex expressions. Parentheses () can be used to control the order of operations.

Example:

GDScript

```
var score: int = 75

var has_powerup: bool = true

if score > 50 and has_powerup:

    print("Player gets a bonus!")

var is_game_over: bool = (score <= 0) or not has_powerup
```

Understanding these operators is crucial for controlling the flow of your game logic and making decisions based on different conditions. They are fundamental tools that you'll use constantly in GDScript.

Chapter 3

Control Flow: Making Decisions and Repeating Actions

Control flow is all about determining the order in which your code is executed. It allows your programs to make decisions based on different conditions and repeat actions as needed. This chapter covers conditional statements (if, elif, else), looping (for and while loops), and the break and continue statements.

3.1 Conditional Statements: if, elif, else

Conditional statements are the backbone of decision-making in your code. They allow your program to execute different blocks of code depending on whether a certain condition is true or false. In GDScript, you use if, elif (short for "else if"), and else to create these conditional structures.

if **statement:** The if statement is the most basic form of a conditional. It executes a block of code *only if* a specified condition is true.

GDScript

```
var player_health = 100

if player_health > 0:

    print("Player is alive!")
```

- In this example, the message "Player is alive!" will only be printed if the player_health variable is greater than 0.
- **else statement:** The else statement provides an alternative block of code to execute if the if condition is false. It acts as a catch-all for when the initial condition isn't met.

GDScript

```
var player_health = 0

if player_health > 0:

    print("Player is alive!")

else:

    print("Player has died!")
```

- Here, since player_health is 0, the if condition is false, and the code within the else block will be executed, printing "Player has died!".
- **elif statement (else if):** The elif statement allows you to check multiple conditions in a sequence. If the initial if condition is false, the program checks the first elif condition. If that's also false, it checks the next elif, and so on. This provides a way to handle multiple possible scenarios.

GDScript

```
var score = 75

if score >= 90:

    print("Excellent!")

elif score >= 80:

    print("Very Good!")

elif score >= 70:

    print("Good!")

elif score >= 60:

    print("Okay")

else:

    print("Needs Improvement!")
```

- In this example, because score is 75, the third elif condition (score >= 70) is true, so "Good!" will be printed. The subsequent elif and else blocks are skipped.

Important points about conditional statements:

- **Conditions:** The conditions used in if, elif, and else statements are typically *boolean expressions* that evaluate to either true or false. These expressions often use comparison operators (like ==, !=, >, <, >=, <=) or logical operators (and, or, not).
- **Indentation:** In GDScript (like Python), indentation is crucial. The code within each block (the code that gets executed if the

condition is true) must be indented. This indentation is what defines the scope of the block. Use consistent indentation (usually 4 spaces) for readability.

- **Order matters:** The order of elif statements is important. The conditions are checked from top to bottom. Once a condition is true, the corresponding block is executed, and the rest are skipped.
- **Optional else:** The else block is optional. You don't have to include an else if you don't need a default action.

Example combining input and conditions:

GDScript

```
func _process(delta):

    if Input.is_action_just_pressed("ui_accept"): # Check for Enter key press

        print("Player pressed Enter!")

    if Input.is_action_just_released("ui_cancel"): # Check for Escape key release

        print("Player released Escape")
```

Conditional statements are essential for creating dynamic and interactive games. They allow your game to respond to player input, game events, and other changing conditions.

3.2 Looping: for and while loops

Loops are essential control flow structures that allow you to repeat a block of code multiple times. GDScript provides two main types of loops: for loops and while loops.

for loops:

The for loop is ideal for iterating over a sequence of items, such as a range of numbers, the elements of an array, or the characters in a string.

- **Iterating through a range of numbers:** The range() function generates a sequence of numbers.

GDScript

```
for i in range(5): # i will take values 0, 1, 2, 3, 4

    print("Number: " + str(i))
```

- In this example, the loop will execute five times. The variable i will take on the values 0, 1, 2, 3, and 4 in each iteration.
- You can also specify a start and end value for the range, as well as a step:

GDScript

```
for i in range(2, 10, 2): # Start at 2, end before 10, step by 2 (2, 4, 6, 8)

    print("Even Number: " + str(i))
```

- **Iterating through an array:** You can directly iterate over the elements of an array using a for loop.

GDScript

```
var fruits = ["apple", "banana", "cherry"]

for fruit in fruits:

    print("Fruit: " + fruit)
```

- In this case, the fruit variable will take on the values "apple", "banana", and "cherry" in successive iterations.
- **Iterating through a String:** You can iterate over each character in a string:

GDScript

```
var my_string = "Hello"

for char in my_string:

    print("Character: " + char)
```

---

while **loops:**

The while loop continues to execute a block of code as long as a specified condition is true. It's important to ensure that the condition eventually becomes false to avoid an *infinite loop*, where the loop never terminates.

GDScript

```
var count = 0

while count < 5:

    print("Count: " + str(count))

    count += 1 # Increment count to avoid an infinite loop!
```

In this example, the loop will execute as long as count is less than 5. Inside the loop, the value of count is printed, and then count is incremented by 1. This ensures that the loop eventually terminates when count reaches 5.

Choosing between for and while loops:

- Use a for loop when you know in advance how many times you need to iterate (e.g., iterating through a range or an array).
- Use a while loop when you need to repeat a block of code until a certain condition is met, and the number of iterations is not known beforehand.

Example combining loops with other concepts:

GDScript

```
var health = 100

var damage = 10

while health > 0:

    print("Current health: " + str(health))

    health -= damage

    if health <= 0:

        print("Character defeated!")
```

This example simulates a character taking damage until their health reaches zero. It uses a while loop to repeat the damage calculation and a conditional statement (if) to check if the character has been defeated.

Understanding and using loops effectively is essential for creating dynamic and interactive games. They are a fundamental tool in any programmer's arsenal.

3.3 Using break and continue statements

The break and continue statements are powerful tools for controlling the flow of loops in GDScript. They allow you to alter the normal execution of a loop based on specific conditions.

break statement:

The break statement is used to immediately exit a loop. When a break statement is encountered inside a loop (either a for or a while loop), the loop terminates immediately, and the program continues executing the code that follows the loop.

GDScript

```
for i in range(10):

    if i == 5:

        break # Exit the loop when i is 5

    print("Number: " + str(i))

print("Loop finished.") # This line will always execute
```

In this example, the loop will print numbers from 0 to 4. When i becomes 5, the break statement is executed, and the loop terminates. The message "Loop finished." is then printed.

continue **statement:**

The continue statement is used to skip the rest of the current iteration of a loop and proceed to the next iteration.[1] When a continue statement is encountered,[2] the code below it within the loop's body is skipped for the current iteration, and the loop continues with the next value (in a for loop) or the next check of the condition (in a while loop).

GDScript

```
for i in range(10):
```

```
if i % 2 == 0: # If i is even

    continue # Skip to the next iteration

    print("Number: " + str(i)) # This will only print odd numbers

print("Loop finished.") # This line will always execute
```

In this example, the loop will print only odd numbers from 1 to 9. When i is even, the continue statement is executed, skipping the print() statement for that iteration. The message "Loop finished." is then printed.

Example combining break, continue, and other concepts:

GDScript

```
var enemies = [10, 20, 0, 15, -5, 5] # Array of enemy health values (negative health is an error)

for health in enemies:

    if health <= 0:

        if health < 0:

            print("Error: Invalid health value (negative).")

            break # Stop processing enemies due to error

        print("Enemy is already dead, skipping.")

        continue # Skip to the next enemy

    print("Dealing damage to enemy with health: " + str(health))
```

```
health -= 5 # Reduce enemy health

if health <= 0:

    print("Enemy defeated!")
```

In this more complex example:

- We iterate over an array of enemy health values.
- If an enemy's health is 0 or less:

If health is negative, we print an error message and break out of the loop entirely, as a negative health value likely indicates a bug.

If health is 0, the enemy is simply already dead, so we continue to the next enemy.

- Otherwise, we deal damage to the enemy.
- If the damage reduces the enemy's health to 0 or less, we print a "defeated" message.

This example demonstrates how break and continue can be used to handle different scenarios within a loop and to improve the robustness of your code. Using these statements effectively can make your code cleaner and more efficient.

Part 2: Object-Oriented Programming in GDScript

Chapter 4

Objects and Classes: Building Blocks of GDScript

This chapter dives into the fundamental concepts of objects and classes, which are the cornerstone of OOP.

4.1 Creating and Instantiating Classes

Let's explore how to create and use classes in GDScript. Classes are the blueprints for creating objects, which are the fundamental building blocks of object-oriented programming (OOP).

What is a Class?

A class is a template that defines the properties (data) and methods (actions) that objects of that class will have. Imagine a blueprint for a house: the blueprint defines the layout, number of rooms, and other features. The actual houses built from that blueprint are the objects (or instances) of the house class.

Defining a Class in GDScript:

In GDScript, you define a class using the class keyword, followed by the class name and a colon. The class body is indented.

GDScript

```
class Player:
```

```
var health = 100

var speed = 5

func move():

    print("Player is moving")


func take_damage(damage):

    health -= damage

    print("Player took " + str(damage) + " damage. Health: " + str(health))
```

Let's break down this Player class:

- class Player:: This line declares a new class named Player. Class names are conventionally capitalized.
- var health = 100: This declares a property (variable) named health and initializes it to 100. Every Player object will have its own health property.
- var speed = 5: This declares a property named speed and initializes it to 5.
- func move():: This defines a method (function) named move(). Methods define the actions an object can perform.
- func take_damage(damage):: This defines a method named take_damage() that takes a damage argument.

Instantiating a Class (Creating an Object):

To create an actual object from a class, you use the new() keyword:

GDScript

```
var my_player = Player.new() # Creates a new Player object
```

Player.new() creates a new *instance* of the Player class. This instance is stored in the my_player variable. Now, my_player is an object, and you can access its properties and call its methods.

Using Objects:

You access properties and call methods using the dot notation (.):

GDScript

```
print(my_player.health) # Accesses the health property (outputs 100)

my_player.speed = 10    # Changes the speed property

my_player.move()        # Calls the move() method (prints "Player is moving")

my_player.take_damage(20) # Calls the take_damage() method (prints "Player took 20 damage. Health: 80")

print(my_player.health) # Accesses the health property again (outputs 80)
```

Example in a script attached to a Node:

Often, you'll define classes within scripts attached to nodes in your Godot scene. This allows the objects you create to interact with the game world.

GDScript

```
extends Node

class Player:

    var health = 100

    var speed = 5

    func move():

        print("Player is moving")

    func take_damage(damage):

        health -= damage

        print("Player took " + str(damage) + " damage. Health: " + str(health))


func _ready():

    var player1 = Player.new()

    player1.move()

    player1.take_damage(20)

    print("Player 1 health: "+ str(player1.health))

    var player2 = Player.new() # Create another player
```

```
print("Player 2 initial health: " + str(player2.health)) # Each instance is independent
```

In this example:

- The Player class is defined within a script that extends Node. This script can be attached to any node in your scene.
- In the _ready() function (which is called when the node enters the scene tree), we create two instances of the Player class: player1 and player2.
- Each instance has its own independent set of properties. Modifying player1.health does not affect player2.health.

This demonstrates the core concepts of creating and instantiating classes in GDScript. It's a fundamental concept in OOP and essential for structuring your game code effectively.

4.2 Properties and Methods: Defining Object Behavior

Properties and methods are what give objects their characteristics and behaviors. They are essential components of classes and define how objects interact and function within your game.

Properties (Data):

Properties are variables that store data associated with an object. They represent the object's attributes or characteristics. In the previous Player class example, health and speed are properties.

You access properties using the dot notation (object.property):

GDScript

```
var my_player = Player.new()

print(my_player.health) # Accesses the health property (outputs 100)

my_player.speed = 10    # Changes the speed property

print(my_player.speed) # Outputs 10
```

- my_player.health: This accesses the health property of the my_player object.
- my_player.speed = 10: This *sets* (or modifies) the speed property of the my_player object to 10.

Each object (instance of a class) has its own copy of its properties. Changing a property of one object does not affect the properties of other objects of the same class.

Methods (Actions):

Methods are functions that define the actions an object can perform. They define the object's behavior. In the Player class, move() and take_damage() are methods.

You call methods using the dot notation followed by parentheses (object.method()):

GDScript

```
my_player.move()      # Calls the move() method (prints "Player is moving")

my_player.take_damage(15) # Calls the take_damage() method, passing 15 as an
argument
```

- my_player.move(): This *calls* (or executes) the move() method of the my_player object.
- my_player.take_damage(15): This calls the take_damage() method, and passes the value 15 as an *argument* to the method. Arguments are values that you provide to a method to customize its behavior.

The self Keyword:

Inside a method, you can use the self keyword to refer to the current object. This is essential for accessing the object's own properties from within its methods.

GDScript

```
class Player:

  var health = 100

  func take_damage(damage):

    self.health -= damage # Use self to refer to the object's health

    print("Player took " + str(damage) + " damage. Health: " + str(self.health))
  #Accessing the updated health

  func heal(amount):

    self.health += amount # Use self to refer to the object's health
```

```gdscript
        print("Player healed for " + str(amount) + " health. Health: " + str(self.health))
```

In the take_damage() and heal() methods, self.health refers to the health property of the specific Player object that the method is being called on.

Example demonstrating properties, methods, and self:

GDScript

```gdscript
extends Node

class Player:

    var health = 100

    var name = "Unnamed Player"


    func set_name(new_name):

        self.name = new_name

    func take_damage(damage):

        self.health -= damage

        print(self.name + " took " + str(damage) + " damage. Health: " + str(self.health))

func _ready():

    var player1 = Player.new()

    player1.set_name("Alice")
```

```
var player2 = Player.new()

player2.set_name("Bob")

player1.take_damage(20) # Alice takes damage

player2.take_damage(10) # Bob takes damage
```

This example demonstrates how each Player object has its own health and name. When take_damage() is called on player1, it only affects player1's health, and the output reflects the correct player's name.

Properties and methods are fundamental to OOP and are essential for creating reusable and organized code in your games. They allow you to encapsulate data and behavior within objects, making your code more modular and easier to manage.

4.3 Understanding Object Inheritance

Object inheritance is a powerful concept in object-oriented programming (OOP) that allows you to create new classes based on existing[1] ones. The new class *inherits* the properties and methods of the original class, promoting code reuse and establishing a hierarchical relationship between classes.

The extends Keyword:

In GDScript, you use the extends keyword to indicate inheritance. The syntax is as follows:

GDScript

```
class Subclass extends Superclass:

    # Subclass properties and methods
```

- Subclass: The name of the new class that will inherit from another class.
- extends: The keyword that indicates inheritance.
- Superclass: The name of the existing class that the Subclass will inherit from. This is also called the *parent class* or *base class*.

Example:

Let's say we have a Character class:

GDScript

```
class Character:

    var health = 100

    var speed = 5

    func move():

        print("Character is moving")

    func take_damage(damage):

        health -= damage

        print("Character took " + str(damage) + " damage. Health: " + str(health))
```

Now, we can create a Player class that inherits from Character:

GDScript

```
class Player extends Character:

    var score = 0

    func collect_item():

        score += 10

        print("Player collected an item. Score: " + str(score))
```

The Player class now automatically has the health, speed, move(), and take_damage() from the Character class, in addition to its own property score and method collect_item().

Overriding Methods:

A subclass can *override* a method from its parent class to provide its own specific implementation. This allows you to customize the behavior of inherited methods.

GDScript

```
class Enemy extends Character:

    var damage = 10

    func attack(target):
```

```
        target.take_damage(damage)

        print("Enemy attacked for " + str(damage) + " damage.")

    func move(): # Overrides the move() method from Character

        print("Enemy is chasing the player!")
```

In this example, the Enemy class inherits the move() method from Character, but it overrides it with its own implementation that prints "Enemy is chasing the player!". When you call move() on an Enemy object, the overridden version will be executed, not the original version from Character.

Example demonstrating inheritance and overriding:

GDScript

```
extends Node

class Character:

    var health = 100

    func take_damage(damage):

        health -= damage

        print("Took " + str(damage) + " damage. Health: " + str(health))

    func move():

        print("Character is moving.")
```

```
class Player extends Character:

    var score = 0

    func collect_points(points):

        score += points

        print("Collected " + str(points) + " points. Score: " + str(score))

class Enemy extends Character:

    var attack_damage = 10

    func attack(target):

        target.take_damage(attack_damage)

        print("Enemy attacked for " + str(attack_damage) + " damage.")

    func move(): # Overrides the move method

        print("Enemy is patrolling.")

func _ready():

    var my_player = Player.new()

    var my_enemy = Enemy.new()

    my_player.move() # Output: Character is moving.

    my_enemy.move() # Output: Enemy is patrolling. (Overridden method)

    my_enemy.attack(my_player) # The Enemy attacks the Player

    my_player.collect_points(50)
```

Key Benefits of Inheritance:

- **Code Reuse:** Avoid writing the same code multiple times. Common properties and methods can be defined in a parent class and inherited by subclasses.
- **Organization:** Creates a clear hierarchy of classes, making your code more organized and easier to understand.
- **Extensibility:** Easily add new classes with specific behaviors by inheriting from existing ones.
- **Polymorphism (covered later):** Allows you to treat objects of different classes in a uniform way, as long as they share a common parent class.

Inheritance is a fundamental concept in OOP and plays a crucial role in creating well-structured and maintainable game code. It allows you to model real-world relationships between objects in your game, making your code more intuitive and efficient.

Chapter 5

Signals and Events: Responding to Actions

Signals are a core feature of Godot's architecture, enabling efficient and decoupled communication between objects (nodes). They are essentially events that an object can emit (send out) to notify other objects that something has happened. This chapter explains how to connect to existing signals, create custom signals, and use them for communication between different parts of your game.

5.1 Connecting Signals to Functions (Signal Handlers)

Connecting signals to functions is the core mechanism for responding to events in Godot.[1] When a signal is emitted by a node (meaning an event has occurred), any functions that are connected to that signal will be automatically executed.[2] These functions are often referred to as *signal handlers* or *callback functions*.

There are two primary ways to connect signals: through the Godot editor and through GDScript code.

Connecting Signals in the Editor (Recommended for Simple Connections):

Connecting signals through the editor is generally the easiest and fastest approach, especially for simple connections and for beginners.

1. **Select the Emitter Node:** In the Scene dock, select the node that emits the signal you want to connect to (e.g., a Button, a Timer, an Area2D, etc.). This is the node that *sends* the signal.

2. **Open the Node Dock:** Open the "Node" dock. It's usually located next to the "Inspector" dock. If you can't find it, go to "Dock" in the top menu and check "Node".
3. **Go to the Signals Tab:** In the Node dock, click on the "Signals" tab. This will display a list of all the signals that the selected node can emit.
4. **Find the Signal:** Locate the specific signal you want to connect to in the list (e.g., pressed for a Button, timeout for a Timer, body_entered for an Area2D).
5. **Connect:** Click the "Connect..." button next to the signal. This will open the "Connect Signal" dialog.
6. **Configure the Connection:** In the "Connect Signal" dialog:

Node: Choose the node that contains the function you want to call when the signal is emitted. This is often the same node where your script is attached. If it is, choose self.

Method/Function: Either choose an existing function from the dropdown list or type a new function name. If you type a new name, Godot will automatically create the function in your script.

7. **Connect:** Click the "Connect" button. Godot will automatically add the necessary connection code to your script.

Connecting Signals in GDScript (For More Dynamic Connections):

Connecting signals in GDScript code is more flexible and is necessary for more complex scenarios, such as connecting signals dynamically at runtime.

GDScript

```gdscript
extends Node

func _ready():

    # Get a reference to the Button node. It must be a child of the node this script is attached to.

    var my_button = get_node("Button")

    #Check if the button is found. get_node() returns null if it doesn't exist.

    if my_button:

        # Connect the "pressed" signal to the "on_button_pressed" function.

        my_button.connect("pressed", self, "on_button_pressed")

    else:

        print("Error: Button node not found. Ensure it's a child of this node.")

func on_button_pressed():

    print("Button was pressed!")
```

Explanation of the connect() method:

- my_button.connect("pressed", self, "on_button_pressed"): This is the core of signal connection in code.

"pressed" (String): The name of the signal you want to connect to. This must match the signal name exactly (case-sensitive).

self (Object): The object that contains the function you want to call. self refers to the current script's node. You can also connect to functions in other scripts by getting a reference to that node.

"on_button_pressed" (String): The name of the function (signal handler) that will be executed when the signal is emitted. This function must exist in the object you specified as the second argument (self in this case).

Important Considerations:

- **Node Hierarchy:** When using get_node(), the node you're trying to get a reference to must be a child (or a descendant further down the tree) of the node the script is attached to. If the node is not a child, you'll need to use other methods like get_tree().get_node() to get a reference to it.
- **Signal and Function Names:** Signal and function names are case-sensitive. Make sure they match exactly.
- _ready() **Function:** Connecting signals is typically done in the _ready() function, which is called when the node enters the scene tree and is ready to be used. This ensures that the nodes you're trying to connect to exist.
- **Null Checks:** It's good practice to check if get_node() returns a valid node before attempting to connect a signal. This prevents errors if the node is not found.

By understanding how to connect signals to functions, you can create interactive and responsive game elements. This is a fundamental skill in Godot game development.

5.2 Custom Signals: Creating Your Own Events

Custom signals allow you to define your own events within your scripts, enabling more flexible and organized communication between different parts of your game. This is especially useful for creating reusable components and decoupling different parts of your game logic.

Defining Custom Signals:

You define custom signals using the signal keyword within your script:

GDScript

extends Node

signal player_died # Signal with no arguments

signal item_collected(item_name, item_value) # Signal with arguments

signal health_changed(new_health) # Signal with one argument

- signal player_died: This line declares a signal named player_died. This signal doesn't send any additional data when it's emitted.
- signal item_collected(item_name, item_value): This line declares a signal named item_collected that takes two arguments: item_name (likely a String) and item_value (likely an int or float). When this signal is emitted, these values will be passed to any connected functions.
- signal health_changed(new_health): This declares a signal that sends the new health value.

Emitting Custom Signals:

To send (or *emit*) a custom signal, you use the emit_signal() function:

GDScript

```
extends Node

signal player_died

signal item_collected(item_name, item_value)

signal health_changed(new_health)

var health = 100

func take_damage(damage):

    health -= damage

    emit_signal("health_changed", health) # Emit the health_changed signal with the updated health

    if health <= 0:

        emit_signal("player_died") # Emit the player_died signal

        print("Player has died!")

func collect_item(name, value):

    emit_signal("item_collected", name, value) # Emit the item_collected signal

    print("Collected " + name + " worth " + str(value) + " points!")

func _process(delta):
```

```
if Input.is_action_just_pressed("ui_accept"):

    take_damage(25)

if Input.is_action_just_pressed("ui_select"):

    collect_item("Coin", 10)
```

Explanation:

- emit_signal("player_died"): This line emits the player_died signal. Any functions connected to this signal will be executed.
- emit_signal("item_collected", name, value): This line emits the item_collected signal, passing the name and value variables as arguments to any connected functions.
- emit_signal("health_changed", health): Emits the health_changed signal, passing the updated health value.

Connecting to Custom Signals:

You connect to custom signals in the same way you connect to built-in signals, either through the editor or using the connect() method in GDScript.

Example connecting in GDScript:

```
GDScript

extends Node

func _ready():

    #Get a reference to the Player node.
```

```
var player = get_node("Player")

if player:

    player.connect("player_died", self, "_on_player_died")

    player.connect("item_collected", self, "_on_item_collected")

    player.connect("health_changed", self, "_on_health_changed")

else:

    print("Error: Player node not found")

func _on_player_died():

    print("Game Over!")

func _on_item_collected(item_name, item_value):

    print("Received item: " + item_name + ", Value: " + str(item_value))

func _on_health_changed(new_health):

    print("Player health changed to: " + str(new_health))
```

Example of Connecting in the editor:

1. Select the node that will receive the signal (the node with the script that contains the signal handler functions).
2. Go to the Node tab and select the Signals section.
3. Choose the node that emits the signal.
4. Select the signal you want to connect.
5. Select the method in the script that will handle the signal.

Benefits of Custom Signals:

- **Decoupling:** Objects don't need direct references to each other. They communicate through signals, making your code more modular and easier to maintain.
- **Flexibility:** You can easily add or remove connections without modifying the emitting object.
- **Reusability:** Components can be reused in different parts of your game because they communicate through well-defined events.
- **Clarity:** Signals make your code easier to understand by clearly defining the events that can occur in your game.

Custom signals are a powerful tool for building robust and scalable games in Godot. They promote good coding practices and make it easier to manage complex game logic.

5.3 Using Signals for Communication Between Objects (Decoupling)

Using signals for communication between objects is a key aspect of good software design, especially in game development. It promotes *decoupling*, which means that different parts of your code are less dependent on each other. This makes your code more modular, maintainable, and reusable.

The Problem with Direct Communication (Tight Coupling):

Imagine a scenario where a Player object directly calls a method on a ScoreLabel object to update the score. This creates a *tight coupling* between the two objects:

- The Player needs to have a direct reference to the ScoreLabel.

- If you want to change how the score is displayed (e.g., use a different UI element), you need to modify the Player's code.
- It becomes harder to reuse the Player in other contexts where there might not be a ScoreLabel.

The Solution: Signals (Loose Coupling):

Signals provide a way for objects to communicate indirectly. The Player emits a signal when the score changes, and the ScoreLabel *listens* for that signal and updates its display accordingly. This is *loose coupling*:

- The Player doesn't need to know anything about the ScoreLabel. It just emits a signal.
- You can easily change how the score is displayed or add other objects that react to the score change without modifying the Player's code.
- The Player becomes more reusable.

Example: Score Management with Signals:

Let's illustrate this with a practical example:

1. Scene Setup:

Create a simple scene with the following nodes:

- A Node2D named "GameManager" (this will hold our main game logic).
- A KinematicBody2D named "Player".
- An Area2D named "Coin" (as a child of a Node2D named "Collectables").
- A Label named "ScoreLabel" (as a child of a CanvasLayer).

2. Scripts:

Coin.gd:

GDScript

```
extends Area2D

signal collected(value)

func _on_body_entered(body):

    if body.is_in_group("player"):

        emit_signal("collected", 10) # Emit the signal with the coin's value

        queue_free() # Remove the coin from the scene
```

GameManager.gd:

GDScript

```
extends Node2D

func _ready():

    var player = get_node("Player")

    var score_label = get_node("CanvasLayer/ScoreLabel")

    var collectables = get_node("Collectables")
```

```
for child in collectables.get_children():

    if child.has_signal("collected"):

        child.connect("collected", self, "_on_coin_collected")

    score_label.text = "Score: 0"

func _on_coin_collected(value):

    var current_score = int(get_node("CanvasLayer/ScoreLabel").text.replace("Score: ", ""))

    current_score += value

    get_node("CanvasLayer/ScoreLabel").text = "Score: " + str(current_score)
```

---

3. Configuration:

- Add the "player" group to the Player node.
- Connect the body_entered signal of the Coin to its own _on_body_entered function.
- Attach the scripts to the corresponding nodes.

Explanation:

- The Coin emits the collected signal with a value (10 in this case) when the player enters its area.
- The GameManager connects to the collected signal of all coins in the scene.
- When the signal is emitted, the _on_coin_collected function in the GameManager is called, updating the score.
- The GameManager then updates the ScoreLabel.

Benefits of this approach:

- **Decoupling:** The Coin doesn't need to know about the GameManager or the ScoreLabel. It just emits a signal.
- **Flexibility:** You can easily add more coins or change how the score is displayed without modifying the Coin's code.
- **Reusability:** The Coin can be reused in other scenes without needing to be reconfigured.

Signals are a powerful tool for building loosely coupled and maintainable game code. They are essential for handling events, user input, and communication between different parts of your game. By using signals, you can create more modular, flexible, and scalable games.

Chapter 6

Working with Nodes in Godot

Godot's architecture is based on a tree structure of nodes. Everything in your game, from sprites and cameras to physics bodies and UI elements, is a node. Understanding how these nodes are organized and how to interact with them using GDScript is crucial for game development in Godot.

6.1 The Godot Scene Tree: Understanding Parent-Child Relationships

The Godot Engine organizes everything within a scene using a hierarchical structure called the *scene tree*. This tree is composed of *nodes*, which are the fundamental building blocks of your game. Understanding how these nodes relate to each other is crucial for effective game development in Godot.

Parent-Child Relationships:

The scene tree is based on *parent-child relationships*. Every node (except the root node) has a parent node. A parent node can have multiple child nodes. This creates a hierarchical structure, much like a family tree or a file system with folders and files.

- **Root Node:** At the very top of the scene tree is the *root node*. Every scene has one and only one root node. This node is the ancestor of all other nodes in the scene.
- **Parent Node:** A *parent node* is a node that contains other nodes (its children). It's like a folder in a file system.

- **Child Node:** A *child node* is a node that is contained within a parent node. It's like a file within a folder.
- **Siblings:** Nodes that share the same parent are called *siblings*.

Inheritance and Transformations:

Child nodes *inherit* certain properties from their parent nodes, most notably their *transform*. The transform includes:

- **Position:** The node's location in the scene.
- **Rotation:** The node's rotation.
- **Scale:** The node's size.

This means that if you move, rotate, or scale a parent node, all of its children will also be moved, rotated, or scaled accordingly. This is a powerful feature for creating complex animations and behaviors.

Example:

Let's imagine a simple game scene with a player character:

- **Root Node:** Node2D (This is a common root node for 2D games)
- **Child of** Node2D**:** KinematicBody2D (This node handles the player's physics and movement)
- **Child of** KinematicBody2D**:** Sprite (This node displays the player's image)
- **Child of** KinematicBody2D**:** CollisionShape2D (This node defines the player's collision area)

In this example:

- Node2D is the *parent* of KinematicBody2D.
- KinematicBody2D is the *parent* of both Sprite and CollisionShape2D.

- Sprite and CollisionShape2D are *children* of KinematicBody2D and are therefore *siblings* of each other.

If you move the KinematicBody2D, both the Sprite and the CollisionShape2D will move along with it. This is because they inherit the KinematicBody2D's transform.

Why Parent-Child Relationships Matter:

Understanding parent-child relationships is fundamental to working with Godot because:

- **Organization:** It helps you organize your game's entities and logic in a structured way.
- **Transformations:** It simplifies complex animations and movements by allowing you to control groups of nodes at once.
- **Node Paths:** It's essential for accessing nodes from your scripts, as node paths are based on the tree structure (which will be explained in the next section).
- **Scene Instancing:** It's important for creating reusable scene components that can be instantiated (created as copies) multiple times within your game.

By grasping the concept of the scene tree and parent-child relationships, you'll be well on your way to effectively managing and manipulating your game's elements in Godot.

6.2 Accessing Nodes Using GDScript

Once you understand the scene tree's parent-child relationships, the next step is learning how to access those nodes from your GDScript code. Godot provides several methods to do this, each with its own use cases.

1. get_node(path) **(Most Common):**

This is the most frequently used method for accessing nodes. It takes a *node path* as a string argument. The node path specifies the location of the node within the scene tree.

- **Relative Paths:** These paths start from the node the script is attached to. You specify the path by listing the names of the nodes, separated by forward slashes (/). For example, if your script is attached to a Player node, and the Player has a child node named Sprite, the relative path to the sprite would be "Sprite".

GDScript

extends Node2D # Script attached to a Node2D

func _ready():

  var player_sprite = get_node("Sprite") # Relative path

  if player_sprite: # ALWAYS check if the node exists!

    print("Found the sprite!")

  else:

    print("Sprite not found!")

- **Absolute Paths:** These paths start from the root of the scene tree. You begin the path with /root/. This is useful for accessing nodes anywhere in the scene, regardless of where your script is attached.

GDScript

```
extends Node2D

func _ready():

    var global_music_player = get_node("/root/MusicPlayer") # Absolute path

    if global_music_player:

        print("Found the music player!")

    else:

        print("Music Player not found!")
```

- **Going Up the Tree:** Use ../ to go up one level in the tree (to the parent node). For example, if your script is attached to a Sprite that is a child of Player, you could use ../ to access the Player node:

GDScript

```
extends Sprite

func _ready():

    var player = get_node("../") # Go up to the parent (Player)
```

```
if player:

    print("Found the parent Player!")

else:

    print("Player not found!")
```

---

2. $ (Shorthand for get_node()):

The $ symbol is a shorthand for get_node(), making your code more concise and readable. It works exactly the same way as get_node() but is shorter to type.

GDScript

```
extends Node2D

func _ready():

    var player = $Player # Shorthand for get_node("Player")

    var player_sprite = $Player/Sprite # Shorthand for get_node("Player/Sprite")

    if player_sprite:

        print("Found the sprite!")

    else:

        print("Sprite not found!")
```

---

3. get_parent():

This method returns the parent node of the node the script is attached to.

GDScript

extends Sprite

func _ready():

  var parent_node = get_parent()

  if parent_node:

    print("Parent node: " + parent_node.name)

  ```

**4. `get_children()`:**

This method returns an array containing all the child nodes of the node the script is attached to.

```gdscript

extends Node2D

func _ready():

  for child in get_children():

    print("Child node: " + child.name)

---

**5.** find_node(name, recursive=true):

This method searches for a node by name.

- name: The name of the node to search for (String).
- recursive: A boolean value. If true (the default), the search will include all descendants (children, grandchildren, etc.). If false, it will only search the immediate children.

---

GDScript

extends Node2D

func _ready():

```
var enemy = find_node("Enemy") # Searches recursively

if enemy:

    print("Found an enemy!")

var directChild = find_node("DirectChild", false) #Searches only direct children

if directChild:

    print("Found a direct child!")
```

Important Tips:

- **Always Check for** null**:** get_node() and find_node() can return null if the node is not found. *Always* check the result of these functions before using the returned node to avoid errors. This is demonstrated in the examples above with if player: or if player_sprite:.

- **Node Paths are Case-Sensitive:** Make sure the node names in your paths match the actual node names in your scene tree exactly, including capitalization.
- **Use Relative Paths When Possible:** Relative paths are generally preferred because they are more robust. If you move a part of your scene tree, relative paths will still work as long as the relative positions of the nodes remain the same.

By using these methods, you can effectively navigate and access any node within your Godot scene from your GDScript code. This is essential for controlling and manipulating objects in your game.

6.3 Manipulating Node Properties from Scripts

Once you have a reference to a node using methods like get_node() or $, you can access and modify its properties from your GDScript code. This allows you to dynamically control various aspects of your game objects, such as their position, rotation, scale, visibility, and more.

Accessing and Modifying Properties:

You access and modify node properties using the dot notation (.):

GDScript

```
extends Node2D

func _ready():

   # Get a reference to a Sprite node (replace "Sprite" with the actual path)

   var my_sprite = $Sprite
```

```gdscript
    # Check if the node exists (important!)

    if my_sprite:

        # Manipulate the sprite's properties

        my_sprite.position = Vector2(100, 50)    # Set the position (x: 100, y: 50)

        my_sprite.rotation = PI / 4           # Set the rotation (45 degrees in radians)

        my_sprite.scale = Vector2(2, 0.5)       # Set the scale (x: 2, y: 0.5)

        my_sprite.visible = false          # Hide the sprite

        my_sprite.modulate = Color(1, 0, 0)     # Change the sprite's color to red

        my_sprite.z_index = 1              #Change the draw order of the sprite

        my_sprite.flip_h = true            #Flip the sprite Horizontally

        my_sprite.flip_v = true            #Flip the sprite Vertically

    else:

        print("Sprite not found!")
```

Let's break down the most commonly used properties:

- position **(Vector2):** This property controls the node's position in 2D space. It's a Vector2, which stores two values: x and y coordinates.

GDScript

```gdscript
my_sprite.position = Vector2(100, 50) # Set the position

var current_position = my_sprite.position # Get the current position

print("X: " + str(current_position.x) + ", Y: " + str(current_position.y))
```

- rotation **(float):** This property controls the node's rotation in radians. Remember that 180 degrees is equal to PI radians.

GDScript

```gdscript
my_sprite.rotation = PI / 2 # Rotate 90 degrees
```

- scale **(Vector2):** This property controls the node's scaling. A scale of (1, 1) means no scaling. (2, 2) doubles the size, and (0.5, 0.5) halves the size.

GDScript

```gdscript
my_sprite.scale = Vector2(0.5, 1.5) # Scale to half width and 1.5 times height
```

- visible **(bool):** This property controls whether the node is visible. Set it to true to show the node and false to hide it.

GDScript

```
my_sprite.visible = false # Hide the sprite
```

- modulate **(Color):** This property controls the node's color. You can use the Color class to create different colors.

GDScript

```
my_sprite.modulate = Color(1, 0, 0)      # Red

my_sprite.modulate = Color(0, 1, 0)      # Green

my_sprite.modulate = Color(0, 0, 1)      # Blue

my_sprite.modulate = Color(0.5, 0.5, 0.5) # Gray

my_sprite.modulate = Color(1, 1, 1, 0.5) # White with 50% alpha (transparency
```

- z_index **(int):** This property controls the drawing order of nodes. Nodes with higher z_index values are drawn on top of nodes with lower values. This is important for layering sprites and UI elements.
- flip_h **(bool):** This property flips the node horizontally.
- flip_v **(bool):** This property flips the node vertically.

Example with different node types:

The properties available depend on the node type. For example, a Label node has a text property, while a Sprite has a texture property.

GDScript

```gdscript
#For a label

$Label.text = "New Text"

#For a Sprite

$Sprite.texture = load("res://icon.png") #Loads a texture from your project

#For a Camera2D

$Camera2D.zoom = Vector2(0.5, 0.5) #Zooms out the camera
```

Important Considerations:

- **Node Type:** Make sure you're accessing properties that are relevant to the node's type. Trying to access a property that doesn't exist will result in an error.
- **Data Types:** Pay attention to the data types of the properties. For example, position is a Vector2, rotation is a float, and visible is a bool. Assigning the wrong data type will also cause an error.
- **Null Checks:** Always check if the node reference is valid (not null) before trying to access its properties. This is crucial to prevent errors if the node is not found in the scene tree.

By manipulating node properties from your scripts, you can create dynamic and interactive game experiences. This is one of the most fundamental skills in Godot game development.

Part 3: Game Development with GDScript

Chapter 7

Input Handling: Responding to Player Actions

This chapter covers how to detect and respond to player input, such as keyboard presses, mouse clicks, gamepad input, and touch input. Effective input handling is essential for creating interactive and engaging games.

7.1 Detecting Keyboard and Mouse Input

Detecting keyboard and mouse input is essential for creating interactive games. Godot provides a robust input system through the Input singleton, which allows you to check the state of various input devices. The recommended way to handle input in Godot is by using *actions*, which you define in the Project Settings.[1]

Using Actions (Recommended):

Actions are named input events that you define in the Project Settings (Project -> Project Settings -> Input Map). This approach offers several advantages:

- **Remapping:** Players can easily remap controls without requiring changes to your code.
- **Abstraction:** Your code doesn't need to know the specific physical input (e.g., "Spacebar" or "Left Mouse Button"). It only deals with the named action (e.g., "jump" or "fire").
- **Multiple Inputs per Action:** You can map multiple physical inputs to the same action (e.g., both "Spacebar" and "Gamepad A" can be mapped to the "jump" action).

Here are the key methods of the Input singleton for working with actions:

- Input.is_action_pressed(action_name): Returns true if the specified action is currently being pressed. This is useful for continuous actions like movement or holding down a fire button.
- Input.is_action_just_pressed(action_name): Returns true only on the frame the action was *just* pressed. This is useful for triggering events that should happen only once per press, like jumping or firing a single shot.
- Input.is_action_just_released(action_name): Returns true only on the frame the action was *just* released. This can be useful for actions that trigger on release, such as charging up an attack.
- Input.get_action_strength(action_name): Returns a floating-point value between 0 and 1 representing how much the action is pressed. Useful for analog inputs like joystick axes or pressure-sensitive buttons.

Example (Keyboard and Mouse with Actions):

First, define the following actions in your Input Map:

- move_right: Map this to the Right Arrow key and the D key.
- move_left: Map this to the Left Arrow key and the A key.
- jump: Map this to the Spacebar.
- fire: Map this to the Left Mouse Button.

Then, in your GDScript code:

GDScript

extends Node2D

```
func _process(delta):

    if Input.is_action_pressed("move_right"):

        print("Moving right")

    if Input.is_action_pressed("move_left"):

        print("Moving left")

    if Input.is_action_just_pressed("jump"):

        print("Just jumped!")

    if Input.is_action_just_released("jump"):

        print("Jump key released!")


    if Input.is_action_just_pressed("fire"):

        print("Fired!")
```

Directly Checking Mouse Buttons (Less Recommended):

While using actions is the preferred approach, you can also directly check
the state of mouse buttons using the following methods:

- Input.is_mouse_button_pressed(button): Returns true if the specified
  mouse button is currently pressed. button should be a constant like
  BUTTON_LEFT, BUTTON_RIGHT, BUTTON_MIDDLE, etc.

Mouse Position and Movement:

- Input.get_mouse_position(): Returns the current mouse position as a Vector2 relative to the game viewport.
- Input.get_mouse_delta(): Returns the mouse movement since the last frame as a Vector2. This is useful for mouse look or dragging.

Example (Direct Mouse Input):

GDScript

```
extends Node2D

func _process(delta):

    if Input.is_mouse_button_pressed(BUTTON_LEFT):

        print("Left mouse button pressed at: " + str(Input.get_mouse_position()))

    var mouse_movement = Input.get_mouse_delta()

    if mouse_movement.length() > 0: #Check if the mouse has moved

        print("Mouse moved by: " + str(mouse_movement))
```

Key Differences and Recommendations:

- **Actions vs. Direct Input:** Using actions is strongly recommended for most cases. It provides greater flexibility, maintainability, and allows for easy remapping of controls. Direct input should only be used in very specific situations where actions are not suitable.
- **_process(delta):** Input handling is usually done in the _process(delta) function, which is called every frame.

- **Delta Time** (delta)**:** The delta parameter in _process(delta) represents the time elapsed since the last frame. It's important to use delta when performing actions that should be frame-rate independent, such as movement. We will discuss this in more detail later.

By using actions and the Input singleton effectively, you can create responsive and customizable controls for your Godot games.

7.2 Handling Gamepad and Touch Input

Handling gamepad and touch input is crucial for making your games accessible on a wider range of devices, including consoles, mobile phones, and tablets. Godot provides built-in support for these input methods, allowing you to create cross-platform games with relative ease.

Gamepad Input:

Godot treats gamepads as *joysticks*. You can access gamepad input using the Input singleton, similar to how you handle keyboard and mouse input. The key difference is that you'll be working with joystick IDs, axes, and buttons.

Input.is_joy_button_pressed(joystick_id, button)**:** Checks if a specific button on a given joystick is currently pressed.

joystick_id: The ID of the joystick (usually 0 for the first connected gamepad, 1 for the second, and so on).

button: A constant representing the button (e.g., JOY_BUTTON_0 for the A button on an Xbox controller, JOY_BUTTON_1 for the B button, JOY_BUTTON_START, JOY_BUTTON_DPAD_UP, etc.). You can find a full list of these constants in the Godot documentation.

Input.get_joy_axis(joystick_id, axis): Gets the value of a specific axis on a given joystick.[1]

joystick_id: The ID of the joystick.

axis: A constant representing the axis (e.g., JOY_AXIS_0 for the left stick's horizontal axis, JOY_AXIS_1 for the left stick's vertical axis, JOY_AXIS_2 for the right stick's horizontal axis, JOY_AXIS_3 for the right stick's vertical axis, JOY_AXIS_6 for the left trigger, JOY_AXIS_7 for the right trigger).

-
- **Using Actions for Gamepads (Recommended):** Just like with keyboard and mouse input, it's highly recommended to use *actions* for gamepad input. This allows for easy remapping and better code organization.

Example (Gamepad Input with Actions):

First, define the following actions in your Input Map:

- move_horizontal: Map this to the left stick's horizontal axis (JOY_AXIS_0).
- jump: Map this to the gamepad's A button (JOY_BUTTON_0).
- fire: Map this to the right trigger (JOY_AXIS_7).

Then, in your GDScript code:

GDScript

extends Node2D

func _process(delta):

```
var    move_direction    =    Input.get_action_strength("move_horizontal")    -
Input.get_action_strength("ui_left")

if move_direction != 0:

    print("Moving horizontally: " + str(move_direction))

if Input.is_action_just_pressed("jump"):

    print("Gamepad Jump!")


var fire_strength = Input.get_action_strength("fire")

if fire_strength > 0:

    print("Firing with strength: " + str(fire_strength))
```

Touch Input (Mobile Devices):

Godot provides support for touch input, making it possible to create games for mobile devices.[2]

- Input.is_touch_screen(): Returns true if the device has a touch screen. This is useful for checking if touch input is available before trying to use it.
- Input.get_touch(index): Returns a TouchEvent object containing information about a specific touch event.
    - index: The index of the touch (0 for the first touch, 1 for the second, and so on).
- Input.get_touch_count(): Returns the number of currently active touch points.

The TouchEvent object has the following properties:

- position (Vector2): The position of the touch on the screen.
- pressed (bool): true if the touch is currently pressed.
- index (int): The index of the touch.

Example (Touch Input):

GDScript

extends Node2D

func _process(delta):

  if Input.is_touch_screen():

    var touch_count = Input.get_touch_count()

    for i in range(touch_count):

      var touch = Input.get_touch(i)

      if touch.pressed:

        print("Touch " + str(touch.index) + " at: " + str(touch.position))

Important Considerations:

- **Input Mapping for Gamepads:** Using actions for gamepad input is highly recommended. It simplifies handling different gamepad layouts and allows for easy remapping.
- **Multi-touch:** Godot supports multi-touch input, allowing you to handle multiple simultaneous touches on a touch screen.[3]

- **Touch Input on Desktop:** On desktop platforms, mouse clicks are reported as touch events with an index of 0. This can be useful for testing touch input on your computer.
- _input(event)**:** For more advanced input handling, especially for handling input events that are not actions (like mouse motion or raw key presses), you can use the _input(event) function. This function receives an InputEvent object that contains detailed information about the input event.

By understanding how to handle gamepad and touch input, you can create games that are playable on a wider range of devices and provide a more intuitive and engaging player experience. Using actions for gamepad input is a best practice that will make your code more maintainable and flexible.

7.3 Creating Custom Input Maps

Creating custom input maps is a crucial step in making your Godot games flexible and user-friendly. Input maps allow you to define named *actions* and then map various physical inputs (keyboard keys, mouse buttons, gamepad buttons, touch events) to those actions. This provides a layer of abstraction that makes it easy to change controls without modifying your game's code.

Accessing the Input Map:

You can access the Input Map in the Project Settings:

1. Open your project in Godot.
2. Go to "Project" -> "Project Settings..." in the top menu.
3. In the Project Settings window, select the "Input Map" tab.

Creating New Actions:

1. In the Input Map tab, you'll see a list of existing actions (if any) and an "Add..." button.
2. Click the "Add..." button.
3. A dialog will appear asking you to enter the name of the new action. Choose a descriptive name (e.g., "move_left," "jump," "fire," "interact"). Action names should be unique.
4. Click "OK." The new action will be added to the list.

Mapping Inputs to Actions:

Once you've created an action, you can map physical inputs to it:

1. Select the action you want to map inputs to in the Input Map list.
2. Click the "+" button below the input list for that action.
3. A dropdown menu will appear with different input types:
   o **Key:** For keyboard keys.
   o **Mouse Button:** For mouse buttons.
   o **Joystick Button:** For gamepad buttons.
   o **Joystick Axis:** For gamepad analog sticks and triggers.
   o **Touchscreen:** For touch events.
4. Select the appropriate input type.
5. Depending on the input type, you'll be presented with different options:
   o **Key:** Press the key you want to map.
   o **Mouse Button:** Click the mouse button you want to map.
   o **Joystick Button:** Press the button on your gamepad.
   o **Joystick Axis:** Move the analog stick or trigger. You'll need to configure the deadzone and other settings for axes.
   o **Touchscreen:** Select the type of touch input.
6. The input will be added to the action's input list. You can add multiple inputs to the same action.

Example: Setting up Movement and Jump:

Let's create a simple example of setting up movement and jump controls:

1. **Create Actions:** In the Input Map, create the following actions:
   - move_left
   - move_right
   - jump
2. **Map Inputs:**
   - Map move_left to the Left Arrow key and the A key.
   - Map move_right to the Right Arrow key and the D key.
   - Map jump to the Spacebar and the Gamepad A button (JOY_BUTTON_0).

Using Actions in GDScript:

Now that you've defined your actions in the Input Map, you can use them in your GDScript code:

```gdscript
GDScript

extends KinematicBody2D

export var speed = 200

func _physics_process(delta):

    var move_direction = 0

    if Input.is_action_pressed("move_right"):

        move_direction += 1

    if Input.is_action_pressed("move_left"):
```

```
    move_direction -= 1

var velocity = Vector2(move_direction * speed, 0)

velocity = move_and_slide(velocity)


if Input.is_action_just_pressed("jump") and is_on_floor():

    velocity.y = -400

    velocity = move_and_slide(velocity)
```

Key Advantages of Using Input Maps:

- **User Customization:** Players can remap controls to their preferences without needing to edit any code.
- **Code Maintainability:** If you need to change a control, you only need to change it in the Input Map, not in multiple places in your code.
- **Abstraction:** Your code works with abstract actions, not specific physical inputs, making it more flexible and easier to understand.
- **Multiple Inputs per Action:** You can easily support multiple input methods (keyboard, gamepad, touch) for the same action.

By using custom input maps, you create a more robust, user-friendly, and maintainable input system for your Godot games. It's a best practice that you should always follow.

Chapter 8

Game Logic and Mechanics: Implementing Gameplay

This chapter focuses on putting the previous concepts together to create actual gameplay. We'll cover game loops, timers, basic game mechanics (like movement and collisions), and managing game state.

8.1 Creating Game Loops and Timers

Creating effective game loops and using timers are fundamental to game development. They control the flow of time and events within your game. Godot provides two primary game loop functions and a Timer node to handle timed events.

Game Loop Functions:

Godot provides two main functions that are called repeatedly during the game's execution:

_process(delta): This function is called every frame. It's the primary place to put code that needs to be updated continuously, such as:

- Handling input.
- Updating animations.
- Updating game logic that doesn't involve physics.
- General game state updates.
- The delta parameter is a crucial element. It represents the time elapsed (in seconds) since the last frame. Using delta ensures that your game logic runs consistently regardless of the frame rate.

GDScript

```
extends Node2D

func _process(delta):

    # Example: Move an object based on input (frame-rate independent)

    var movement = 100 * delta # Movement speed * time since last frame

    position.x += movement * Input.get_action_strength("ui_right")

    position.x -= movement * Input.get_action_strength("ui_left")

    #Print the delta time each frame

    print("Delta time: " + str(delta))
```

_physics_process(delta): This function is called at a fixed rate (usually 60 times per second by default). It's specifically designed for physics calculations and any logic that needs to be synchronized with the physics engine. Use this for:

- Movement of KinematicBody2D and RigidBody2D nodes.
- Collision detection and handling.
- Other physics-related calculations.
- Like _process(), _physics_process() also receives the delta parameter, which represents the fixed timestep used for physics calculations.

GDScript

```
extends KinematicBody2D

export var speed = 200

func _physics_process(delta):

    var velocity = Vector2.ZERO

    if Input.is_action_pressed("ui_right"):

        velocity.x = 1

    if Input.is_action_pressed("ui_left"):

        velocity.x = -1

    velocity = velocity.normalized() * speed

    velocity = move_and_slide(velocity)
```

Choosing between _process() **and** _physics_process():

- Use _process() for general game logic, input handling, and animations that don't directly involve physics.
- Use _physics_process() for physics-related calculations and movement of physics bodies.

Timers (Timer Node):

The Timer node provides a convenient way to trigger events after a certain amount of time has passed.

1. **Add a Timer Node:** Add a Timer node as a child of the node where you want to use it.

2. **Set** Wait Time**:** In the Inspector panel of the Timer node, set the Wait Time property to the desired duration in seconds.
3. **Connect the** timeout **Signal:** Connect the timeout signal of the Timer to a function in your script. This function will be called when the timer finishes.
4. **Start and Stop the Timer:** Use the start() and stop() methods of the Timer to control when the timer is running.
5. **One Shot:** The One Shot property determines if the timer will stop automatically after timing out once (true) or if it will repeat continuously (false).

Example using Timer**:**

GDScript

extends Node2D

func _ready():

   # Get the timer node (using the $ shorthand)

   $Timer.connect("timeout", self, "_on_timer_timeout")

   $Timer.start() # Start the timer

func _on_timer_timeout():

   print("Timer timed out!")

   $Timer.start() # Restart the timer for continuous timing

   #Or remove the line above if you set the timer to One Shot in the editor

---

Example using Timer **with a delay and one shot:**

GDScript

```
extends Node2D

func _ready():

    # Get the timer node (using the $ shorthand)

    $Timer.wait_time = 2 #Set wait time to 2 seconds

    $Timer.one_shot = true #Set the timer to only run once

    $Timer.connect("timeout", self, "_on_timer_timeout")

    $Timer.start() # Start the timer

func _on_timer_timeout():

    print("Timer timed out after 2 seconds!")
```

Combining _process **and** Timer**:**

You can use both _process() and Timer nodes in the same script. _process() handles continuous updates, while Timer nodes handle specific timed events.

Understanding game loops and timers is crucial for creating dynamic and interactive games. Using delta time ensures frame-rate independence, and Timer nodes provide a clean way to manage timed events.

8.2 Implementing Basic Game Mechanics (e.g., Movement, Collisions)

Implementing basic game mechanics like movement and collisions is fundamental to creating interactive gameplay. Godot provides several tools and nodes to handle these mechanics efficiently. This section focuses on using KinematicBody2D for movement and Area2D for collision detection.

Movement (KinematicBody2D):

The KinematicBody2D node is designed for character movement and simple collision handling. It's particularly well-suited for platformers, top-down games, and other games where you need precise control over movement and basic collision responses.

Key methods and properties:

move_and_slide(linear_velocity, up_direction = Vector2(0, -1)): This is the primary method for moving a KinematicBody2D.

linear_velocity (Vector2): The desired movement velocity (direction and speed).

up_direction (Vector2): The "up" direction. This is important for determining what constitutes a "floor" for jumping and other gravity-related calculations. For 2D games where up is typically -Y, use Vector2(0, -1).

- is_on_floor(): Returns true if the body is currently standing on a floor.
- is_on_wall(): Returns true if the body is currently colliding with a wall.

- **is_on_ceiling():** Returns true if the body is currently colliding with a ceiling.

Example (Basic Movement):

GDScript

```
extends KinematicBody2D

export var speed = 200

export var jump_force = -400

var velocity = Vector2.ZERO

func _physics_process(delta):

    velocity.x = 0 # Reset horizontal velocity each frame

    var move_direction = Input.get_action_strength("ui_right") - Input.get_action_strength("ui_left")

    velocity.x = move_direction * speed

    if Input.is_action_just_pressed("ui_up") and is_on_floor():

        velocity.y = jump_force

    velocity.y += 980 * delta # Apply gravity

    velocity = move_and_slide(velocity, Vector2(0, -1))
```

Explanation:

1. velocity.x = 0: Reset the horizontal velocity at the beginning of each frame to prevent accumulating speed.
2. move_direction: Calculates the horizontal movement direction based on input.
3. velocity.x = move_direction * speed: Sets the horizontal velocity.
4. if Input.is_action_just_pressed("ui_up") and is_on_floor():: Checks for jump input and if the player is on the floor.
5. velocity.y = jump_force: Applies the jump force.
6. velocity.y += 980 * delta: Applies gravity.
7. velocity = move_and_slide(velocity, Vector2(0, -1)): Moves the KinematicBody2D and handles collisions.

Collisions (Area2D):

The Area2D node is used for detecting overlaps between objects. It doesn't handle physics simulations like KinematicBody2D or RigidBody2D; it simply detects when other physics bodies enter or exit its area.

Key signals:

- body_entered(body): Emitted when a physics body enters the Area2D.
- body_exited(body): Emitted when a physics body exits the Area2D.
- area_entered(area): Emitted when another Area2D enters this Area2D.
- area_exited(area): Emitted when another Area2D exits this Area2D.

Example (Collecting Items):

Suppose you have a "Coin" scene with an Area2D as its root node. You want the player to collect the coin when they overlap with it.

Coin.gd:

GDScript

```
extends Area2D

signal collected

func _on_body_entered(body):
    if body.is_in_group("player"): # Check if the entering body is in the "player" group
        emit_signal("collected")
        queue_free() # Remove the coin from the scene
```

Player.gd:

GDScript

```
extends KinematicBody2D

func _ready():
    for child in get_tree().get_nodes_in_group("coins"):
        child.connect("collected", self, "_on_coin_collected")

func _on_coin_collected():
    print("Coin collected!")
    Global.score += 10 #Update global score
```

```
print("Score: " + str(Global.score))
```

Explanation:

1. The Coin's Area2D emits the collected signal when a body in the "player" group enters its area.
2. The Player connects to the collected signal of all coins in the scene.
3. When the signal is emitted, the _on_coin_collected() function in the Player is called.

Using Groups:

Using groups is a good way to identify different types of nodes. You can add nodes to groups in the editor's Node tab. In the above example, we check if the entering body is in the "player" group using body.is_in_group("player").

By combining KinematicBody2D for movement and Area2D for collisions, you can implement a wide range of game mechanics in your Godot projects. Remember to use the delta parameter for frame-rate-independent calculations and use groups for better organization.

8.3 Managing Game State and Data

Managing game state and data is essential for creating complex and engaging games. It involves storing, updating, and retrieving information that represents the current state of your game world. Godot provides several ways to handle this, from simple variables to more advanced techniques like singletons (autoloads) and saving/loading data.

1. Variables (Local and Instance):

- **Local Variables:** These variables are declared within a function and are only accessible within that function. They are used for temporary storage within a specific scope.

GDScript

```
func _ready():

    var message = "Hello, world!" # Local variable

    print(message)

func another_function():

    # print(message) # This would cause an error, as 'message' is not defined in this scope.

    pass
```

- **Instance Variables (Properties):** These variables are declared within a class (but outside any function) and are associated with each instance (object) of that class. They store the object's state.

GDScript

```
extends Node2D

export var speed = 200 # Visible in the editor

var health = 100      # Not visible in the editor

var score = 0
```

```
func take_damage(damage):

    health -= damage

    if health <= 0:

        queue_free()

func add_score(points):

    score += points

    print("Score: " + str(score))
```

---

2. Singletons (Autoloads):

Singletons (or autoloads) are global objects that are automatically loaded when your game starts and remain in memory for the entire duration of the game. They are ideal for storing global game data that needs to be accessible from anywhere in your project, such as:

- Player stats (score, lives, inventory).
- Game settings (volume, difficulty).
- Global game state (current level, game over status).

To create an autoload:

1. Create a new script (e.g., Global.gd).
2. In the Project Settings (Project -> Project Settings... -> Autoload), add the script. Give it a name (e.g., "Global").

Now you can access the variables and functions in your autoload from any script using its name:

Global.gd:

```gdscript
GDScript

extends Node

var score = 0

var player_name = "Player 1"

var game_over = false


func reset_game():

  score = 0

  game_over = false
```

Any other script:

```gdscript
GDScript

func _ready():

  Global.score += 10 # Access the global score

  print("Global Score: " + str(Global.score))

  print("Player name: " + Global.player_name)

func _process(delta):
```

```
if Global.game_over:

    print("Game Over!")
```

---

3. Saving and Loading Data:

For persistent data that needs to be saved between game sessions, you can use Godot's built-in file I/O capabilities.

```
GDScript

# Saving data

func save_game():

  var save_data = {

    "score": Global.score,

    "player_name": Global.player_name

  }

  var file = File.new()

  file.open("user://savegame.json", File.WRITE) # user:// is the user data directory

  file.store_line(JSON.print(save_data))

  file.close()

  print("Game Saved")

# Loading data
```

```
func load_game():

  var file = File.new()

  if file.file_exists("user://savegame.json"):

    file.open("user://savegame.json", File.READ)

    var json_string = file.get_as_text()

    var save_data = JSON.parse(json_string).result

    file.close()

    Global.score = save_data["score"]

    Global.player_name = save_data["player_name"]

    print("Game Loaded")

  else:

    print("No save file found.")
```

Explanation:

- user://: This is a special path that refers to the user data directory, where you should store save files.
- JSON.print(): Converts a GDScript dictionary to a JSON string for saving.
- JSON.parse(): Parses a JSON string back into a GDScript dictionary.
- Error Handling: It's important to include error handling (e.g., checking if the file exists) when loading data.

Example combining concepts:

GDScript

```
extends Node2D

func _ready():

    Global.score = 0

    load_game()

func _process(delta):

    if Input.is_action_just_pressed("ui_accept"):

        Global.score += 10

        print("Score: " + str(Global.score))

        save_game()

func save_game():

    # ... (same as above)

func load_game():

    # ... (same as above)
```

By using these techniques, you can effectively manage the state and data of your Godot games, creating more complex and engaging experiences.

Using singletons for global data and saving/loading for persistent data are best practices that will make your code more organized and maintainable.

Chapter 9

User Interfaces (UI): Creating In-Game Menus

This chapter covers creating user interfaces (UIs) for your games, specifically focusing on in-game menus. Godot's UI system is based on Control nodes, which provide a flexible and powerful way to create complex and interactive interfaces.

9.1 Using Control Nodes for UI Elements

Control nodes are the foundation of Godot's UI system. They are specifically designed for creating user interfaces and are not rendered in the 3D or 2D game world like regular Node2D or Spatial nodes. Instead, they are drawn on top of the viewport.

Key Characteristics of Control Nodes:

- **Rectangular:** Control nodes are rectangular and are positioned and sized using their rect property (which includes properties like position, size, anchor, and margin).
- **Anchors and Margins:** These are crucial for positioning and sizing Control nodes relative to their parent. Anchors define the reference point (e.g., top-left, bottom-right, center), and margins define the offset from that point.
- **Containers:** Container nodes (like VBoxContainer, HBoxContainer, GridContainer) automatically arrange their child Control nodes, simplifying UI layout and making it responsive to different screen sizes.
- **CanvasLayer:** Control nodes are usually placed within a CanvasLayer. This allows you to create separate UI layers (e.g., a HUD that always stays on top of the game world).

Common Control **Nodes:**

Here are some of the most frequently used Control nodes:

- Label: Displays text. Key properties include text, align, valign (vertical alignment), autowrap, and clip_text.

GDScript

```
$MyLabel.text = "Hello, Godot!"

$MyLabel.align = Label.ALIGN_CENTER
```

- Button: Creates clickable buttons. The most important signal is pressed, which is emitted when the button is clicked.

GDScript

```
$MyButton.text = "Click Me!"

$MyButton.connect("pressed", self, "_on_button_pressed")

func _on_button_pressed():

  print("Button was clicked!")
```

- LineEdit: Creates a single-line text input field. Useful properties include text, placeholder_text, and signals like text_changed and text_entered.

GDScript

```
$MyLineEdit.placeholder_text = "Enter your name"

print($MyLineEdit.text) #Get the current text
```

- TextureRect: Displays an image (texture). Key properties include texture, stretch_mode, and expand.

GDScript

```
$MyTextureRect.texture = load("res://icon.png") # Load a texture from your project
```

- Panel: Creates a simple background panel. Useful for grouping UI elements and providing visual separation.
- VBoxContainer: Arranges child nodes vertically.
- HBoxContainer: Arranges child nodes horizontally.
- GridContainer: Arranges child nodes in a grid.

Anchors and Margins in Detail:

Anchors and margins work together to position and size Control nodes.

- **Anchors:** Anchors are normalized values (between 0 and 1) that define the reference point within the parent Control node. The anchors represent the relative position within the parent for the control's top left, top right, bottom left, and bottom right corners.
- **Margins:** Margins are pixel offsets from the anchor points.

Here's how they work together:

1. The anchor positions are multiplied by the parent's size to get pixel coordinates within the parent.
2. The margins are then added to these pixel coordinates to determine the final position and size of the Control node.

Example:

If a Control node has anchors set to (0, 0, 1, 1) (meaning it stretches to fill its parent) and margins set to (10, 10, -10, -10), it will be positioned 10 pixels from the left and top edges of its parent and 10 pixels from the right and bottom edges of its parent.

Using Containers for Layout:

Container nodes are essential for creating flexible and responsive UIs. They automatically arrange their child Control nodes based on their type and properties.

- VBoxContainer: Arranges children vertically. You can control the spacing between children using the separation property.
- HBoxContainer: Arranges children horizontally. You can control the spacing between children using the separation property.
- GridContainer: Arranges children in a grid. You can control the number of columns using the columns property.

Example (Using VBoxContainer):

1. Add a VBoxContainer to your scene.
2. Add several Button nodes as children of the VBoxContainer.

The VBoxContainer will automatically arrange the buttons vertically with even spacing.

By understanding how to use Control nodes, anchors, margins, and containers, you can create complex and adaptable user interfaces for your Godot games. This is a crucial skill for creating user-friendly and visually appealing games.

9.2 Creating Interactive Menus and Buttons

Creating interactive menus and buttons is a core part of UI design in games. Godot's Button node, combined with signals, makes this process straightforward.

The Button Node:

The Button node is the primary UI element for creating clickable buttons. It inherits from Control, so it has all the standard Control properties (like rect_position, rect_size, anchor, margin), but it also has some specific properties and signals:

- text **(String):** The text displayed on the button.
- icon **(Texture):** An optional icon displayed on the button.
- flat **(bool):** If true, the button will not have a visual border or background by default.
- **Signals:** The most important signal is pressed, which is emitted when the button is clicked or tapped.

Creating Buttons in the Editor:

1. **Add a Button Node:** In your scene, add a Button node as a child of a CanvasLayer or other suitable Control node (like a VBoxContainer for arranging multiple buttons).
2. **Set the Text:** In the Inspector panel, set the text property to the text you want to display on the button (e.g., "Start Game," "Options," "Quit").

3. **(Optional) Set an Icon:** If you want to display an icon on the button, drag a Texture resource to the icon property in the Inspector.
4. **Position and Size:** Adjust the rect_position and rect_size or use anchors and margins to position and size the button as needed.

Connecting Signals to Functions (Signal Handlers):

To make the button interactive, you need to connect its pressed signal to a function in your script. This function will be executed when the button is clicked.

Connecting Signals in the Editor (Easiest Method):

1. Select the Button node in the Scene dock.
2. Go to the "Node" dock and select the "Signals" tab.
3. Find the pressed signal in the list.
4. Click the "Connect..." button.
5. In the "Connect Signal" dialog:

Select the node that contains the script with the function you want to call (usually the same node that contains the button or a parent node).

Choose an existing function or type a new name for the function (e.g., _on_start_button_pressed).

6. Click "Connect." Godot will automatically generate the connection code in your script.

Connecting Signals in GDScript:

You can also connect signals directly in your script using the connect() method:

GDScript

```gdscript
extends CanvasLayer # Or any other Control node

func _ready():

    # Get a reference to the button (using the $ shorthand)

    $StartButton.connect("pressed", self, "_on_start_button_pressed")

    $QuitButton.connect("pressed", self, "_on_quit_button_pressed")


func _on_start_button_pressed():

    print("Start button clicked!")

    # Load the game scene

    get_tree().change_scene("res://game.tscn")

func _on_quit_button_pressed():

    print("Quit button clicked!")

    get_tree().quit()
```

Creating a Simple Menu:

Let's create a basic main menu with "Start Game" and "Quit" buttons:

1. Create a new scene (e.g., main_menu.tscn).
2. Add a CanvasLayer as the root node.

3. Add a VBoxContainer as a child of the CanvasLayer. This will arrange the buttons vertically.
4. Add two Button nodes as children of the VBoxContainer.
5. Set the text property of the buttons to "Start Game" and "Quit."
6. Connect the pressed signals of the buttons to functions in a script attached to the CanvasLayer (as shown in the previous GDScript example).

Example with button states:

GDScript

```
extends CanvasLayer

func _ready():

    $MyButton.connect("pressed", self, "_on_button_pressed")

    $MyButton.connect("mouse_entered", self, "_on_mouse_entered")

    $MyButton.connect("mouse_exited", self, "_on_mouse_exited")

func _on_button_pressed():

    print("Button Pressed")

    $MyButton.text = "Pressed!"

func _on_mouse_entered():

    $MyButton.text = "Hovering"

func _on_mouse_exited():

    $MyButton.text = "Click me!"
```

By using the Button node and connecting its pressed signal, you can easily create interactive menus and buttons for your Godot games. Using containers like VBoxContainer and HBoxContainer helps you create organized and responsive layouts.

9.3 Scripting UI Behavior

Scripting UI behavior involves using GDScript to control the behavior and appearance of your UI elements dynamically. This allows you to create interactive menus, respond to user input, update UI elements based on game events, and much more.

Accessing UI Elements from Scripts:

First, you need to get a reference to the Control nodes you want to manipulate. You can do this using get_node() or the $ shorthand, just like with other nodes:

GDScript

```
extends CanvasLayer


func _ready():

    var my_label = get_node("MyLabel") # Using get_node()

    var my_button = $MyButton      # Using the $ shorthand

    if my_label: # Always check if the node exists!
```

```
    print("Label found!")

else:

    print("Label not found!")

if my_button:

    print("Button found!")

else:

    print("Button not found!")
```

Manipulating UI Properties:

Once you have a reference to a Control node, you can access and modify its properties. Here are some commonly used properties:

- text **(String):** For Label and Button nodes, this property sets or gets the displayed text.

GDScript

```
$MyLabel.text = "New Text!"

$MyButton.text = "Click Me Again!"
```

- visible **(bool):** Controls the visibility of the node.

GDScript

```
$MyPanel.visible = true  # Show the panel

$MyPanel.visible = false # Hide the panel
```

- disabled **(bool):** Disables or enables a Control node, preventing user interaction.

GDScript

```
$MyButton.disabled = true  # Disable the button

$MyButton.disabled = false # Enable the button
```

- modulate **(Color):** Changes the node's color. This affects text color for Label and Button nodes and the overall color for other Control nodes.

GDScript

```
$MyLabel.modulate = Color(1, 0, 0) # Red text
```

- rect_position **(Vector2),** rect_size **(Vector2),** rect_scale **(Vector2):** These properties control the node's position, size, and scale. Using anchors and margins is usually preferred for layout, but you can use these for dynamic changes.

Responding to UI Events (Signals):

The most common way to make UI elements interactive is by connecting signals to functions.

GDScript

```
extends CanvasLayer


func _ready():

    $StartButton.connect("pressed", self, "_on_start_pressed")

    $OptionsButton.connect("pressed", self, "_on_options_pressed")

    $QuitButton.connect("pressed", self, "_on_quit_pressed")

    $MyLineEdit.connect("text_changed", self, "_on_text_changed")

    $MyLineEdit.connect("text_entered", self, "_on_text_entered")

func _on_start_pressed():

    print("Start button pressed!")

    # Load the game scene

    get_tree().change_scene("res://game.tscn")

func _on_options_pressed():

    print("Options button pressed!")

    # Open options menu
```

```gdscript
$OptionsMenu.visible = true

func _on_quit_pressed():

    print("Quit button pressed!")

    get_tree().quit()

func _on_text_changed(new_text):

    print("Line Edit text changed: " + new_text)

func _on_text_entered(new_text):

    print("Line Edit text entered: " + new_text)
```

Example: Showing and Hiding UI Elements:

GDScript

```gdscript
extends CanvasLayer

func _ready():

    $ShowButton.connect("pressed", self, "_on_show_pressed")

    $HideButton.connect("pressed", self, "_on_hide_pressed")

    $MyPanel.visible = false # Initially hide the panel

func _on_show_pressed():

    $MyPanel.visible = true
```

```gdscript
func _on_hide_pressed():

    $MyPanel.visible = false
```

Example: Changing UI based on Game State:

GDScript

```gdscript
extends CanvasLayer

func _process(delta):

    if Global.game_over: # Check a global game state variable

        $GameOverLabel.visible = true

        $ScoreLabel.visible = false

    else:

        $GameOverLabel.visible = false

        $ScoreLabel.text = "Score: " + str(Global.score) # Update the score label
```

Example: Using LineEdit Input:

GDScript

```gdscript
extends CanvasLayer

func _ready():
```

```
$NameInput.connect("text_entered", self, "_on_name_entered")

func _on_name_entered(new_name):

    print("Player entered name: " + new_name)

    Global.player_name = new_name #Store the player name in a Global variable

    $NameInput.clear() #Clear the input field
```

By scripting UI behavior, you can create dynamic and interactive user interfaces that respond to player actions and game events. This is essential for creating engaging and user-friendly games. Remember to always check if the node you are trying to access exists to prevent errors.

Chapter 10

Debugging and Optimization: Improving Your Code

This chapter covers essential techniques for finding and fixing errors in your code (debugging) and improving its performance (optimization). Writing efficient and bug-free code is crucial for creating smooth and enjoyable games.

10.1 Using the Godot Debugger

The Godot debugger is an invaluable tool for finding and fixing errors in your GDScript code. It allows you to pause your game's execution, inspect variables, step through code line by line, and understand the flow of your program.

Key Features of the Godot Debugger:

- **Setting Breakpoints:** A breakpoint pauses the execution of your game when it reaches a specific line of code. This allows you to examine the state of your game at that precise moment.

How to Set a Breakpoint: In the script editor, click on the line number next to the line of code where you want to set the breakpoint. A red dot will appear, indicating that a breakpoint has been set.

Inspecting Variables: When your game is paused at a breakpoint, the "Debugger" dock (usually at the bottom of the Godot editor) becomes active. In the "Locals" or "Members" tab, you can see the current values of variables in the current scope.

Stepping Through Code: The debugger provides controls for stepping through your code:

Step Over (F10): Executes the current line of code and moves to the next line in the *same function*. If the current line is a function call, it executes the entire function without stepping into it.

Step Into (F11): If the current line of code is a function call, it steps *into* that function, allowing you to debug the function's execution.

Step Out (Shift + F11): Finishes executing the current function and returns to the function that called it.

Continue (F5): Resumes normal execution of the game until the next breakpoint is encountered or the game ends.

- **Call Stack:** The "Call Stack" tab in the debugger shows the sequence of function calls that led to the current point of execution. This is extremely helpful for understanding the flow of your program and identifying where errors might have originated.
- **Watches:** You can add "watches" to specific variables to monitor their values as the code executes. This is useful for tracking variables that might change frequently.

How to Add a Watch: In the "Watches" tab of the debugger, click the "+" button and enter the name of the variable you want to watch.

- **Break on Error:** In the debugger settings (accessible through the wrench icon in the debugger dock), you can enable "Break on Error." This will automatically pause execution when a runtime error occurs, making it easier to identify the source of the error.
- **Output Panel:** The "Output" panel displays error messages, print statements (from print() calls in your code), and other output from

your game. This is the first place you should look when encountering issues.

Example Debugging Session:

Let's say you have the following code:

```gdscript
GDScript

extends Node2D

var x = 10

var y = 0

func _ready():

    calculate_result()

    print("Result: " + str(result)) # result is not defined here

func calculate_result():

    var a = x

    var b = y

    var result = a / b # Potential division by zero error

    print("Calculating...")
```

If you run this code, you'll likely get a division by zero error. Here's how you can use the debugger to find the problem:

1. Set a breakpoint on the line var result = a / b.
2. Run the game. Execution will pause at the breakpoint.
3. In the "Locals" tab of the debugger, you'll see that a is 10 and b is 0.
4. This confirms that the division by zero is the cause of the error.
5. You can then modify your code to handle this case (e.g., by adding a check to prevent division by zero).

Workflow Tips:

- **Start with Print Statements:** Before using the full debugger, use print() statements to output the values of key variables. This can often help you quickly identify simple errors.
- **Use Breakpoints Strategically:** Don't set too many breakpoints at once. Focus on the area of your code where you suspect the error is occurring.
- **Inspect Variables Regularly:** When paused at a breakpoint, take the time to inspect the values of relevant variables. This can often give you valuable clues about what's going wrong.
- **Use the Call Stack:** If you're having trouble understanding how your code reached a certain point, use the call stack to trace the function calls.

By mastering the Godot debugger, you'll be able to identify and fix errors in your code much more efficiently, leading to a smoother and more productive development process.

10.2 Common GDScript Errors and How to Fix Them

GDScript, while designed to be beginner-friendly, can still present various errors during development. Understanding these common errors and their solutions is crucial for efficient debugging. This section covers some of the most frequent GDScript errors and how to resolve them.

1. Invalid get index '...' (on base: 'null') / Attempt to call function '...' in base 'null':

These are perhaps the most common errors in GDScript. They occur when you try to access a property or call a method on a node that doesn't exist (the node reference is null).

- **Cause:** This usually happens when get_node() or $ fails to find the specified node, often due to typos in the node path, incorrect scene hierarchy, or trying to access a node before it's ready (e.g., in the _init() function).
- **Solution:** *Always* check if the node reference is valid before using it:

GDScript

```
extends Node2D

func _ready():

    var player = get_node("Player")

    if player != null: # The crucial check

        player.position = Vector2(100, 100)

        player.call_function()
```

```
    else:

        print("Error: Player node not found! Check the node path or scene tree.")

# More concise way to do the same check

func _ready():

    if $Player:

        $Player.position = Vector2(100,100)

    else:

        print("Error: Player node not found! Check the node path or scene tree.")
```

- onready **keyword:** Using onready is a best practice. This keyword initializes the variable when the node enters the scene tree, preventing null errors in _ready():

GDScript

```
onready var player = get_node("Player")

func _ready():

    player.position = Vector2(100, 100) # No need to check for null here
```

---

2. Invalid set index '...' (on base: 'Array') / Index out of range:

These errors occur when you try to access an element of an array using an invalid index (an index that is less than 0 or greater than or equal to the array's size).

- **Cause:** Incorrect loop conditions, typos in index variables, or trying to access an element after removing it from the array.
- **Solution:** Double-check your loop conditions and make sure your index variables are within the valid range:

GDScript

```
var my_array = [10, 20, 30]

var index = 3 # Error: Index out of range (valid indices are 0, 1, 2)


if index >= 0 and index < my_array.size(): #Check if the index is valid

  print(my_array[index])

for i in range(my_array.size()): # Use range to iterate safely

  print(my_array[i])
```

---

3. Type Errors:

GDScript is dynamically typed, but it does perform some type checking at runtime. Type errors occur when you try to perform an operation on a value of an incompatible type (e.g., adding a string to a number).

- **Cause:** Incorrect variable assignments, passing arguments of the wrong type to functions, or using operators that are not defined for the given types.
- **Solution:** Use the typeof() function to check the type of a variable, and use explicit type conversions when necessary:

GDScript

```
var my_variable = "10"

var my_number = int(my_variable) # Convert string to integer

if typeof(my_number) == TYPE_INT:

    print(my_number + 5) # Now this is a valid operation

var my_float = float("3.14")

print(typeof(my_float)) # Output: 2 (TYPE_REAL)
```

---

4. Syntax Errors:

These errors occur when your code violates the GDScript syntax rules.

Cause: Missing colons, incorrect indentation, typos, incorrect use of operators.

Solution: Godot usually highlights syntax errors in the script editor. Carefully review the line where the error is reported and the surrounding code. Common syntax errors include:

- Missing colons at the end of if, for, while, func, class statements.

- Inconsistent indentation (GDScript uses indentation to define code blocks).
- Typos in variable or function names.

5. Connecting Signals to Nonexistent Functions:

If you try to connect a signal to a function that doesn't exist, you'll get an error.

- **Cause:** Typos in the function name when connecting the signal or deleting a function after connecting a signal to it.
- **Solution:** Double-check the function name in the connect() method. If you're connecting in the editor, make sure the function still exists in the script.

General Debugging Tips:

- **Use print() statements:** Use print() liberally to output the values of variables and check the flow of your program.
- **Use the debugger:** The Godot debugger is an invaluable tool for finding and fixing errors. Use breakpoints, variable inspection, and stepping through code to understand what's happening in your program.
- **Read error messages carefully:** Error messages often provide valuable clues about the cause of the error.
- **Check the documentation:** The Godot documentation is a great resource for finding information about GDScript syntax, built-in functions, and node properties.

By understanding these common errors and their solutions, you'll be able to debug your GDScript code more efficiently and create more robust games. Remember to use the debugger and print() statements strategically to track down those pesky bugs!

10.3 Tips for Optimizing GDScript Performance

Optimizing your GDScript code is crucial for creating smooth and performant games, especially as your projects grow in complexity. This section provides several tips and best practices for improving GDScript performance.

1. Minimize get_node() Calls:

get_node() is a relatively expensive operation because it traverses the scene tree. Avoid calling it repeatedly within loops or in _process() if you can.

- **Bad (Repeated get_node()):**

GDScript

```
func _process(delta):

    $Sprite.position.x += 10 * delta

    $Sprite.rotation += 0.1 * delta
```

- **Good (onready and Stored Reference):**

GDScript

```
onready var sprite = $Sprite # onready ensures the node is ready

func _process(delta):

    sprite.position.x += 10 * delta

    sprite.rotation += 0.1 * delta
```

---

2. Use onready for Node References:

The onready keyword ensures that a variable is initialized when the node enters the scene tree and is ready to be used. This prevents potential null errors and is more efficient than initializing in _ready() if the node is a child.

3. Optimize Loops:

- **Avoid Unnecessary Calculations Inside Loops:** If a calculation doesn't depend on the loop index, perform it outside the loop.

GDScript

```
# Bad

var constant_value = 10

for i in range(1000):

    var result = constant_value * 2 # Unnecessary calculation inside the loop

# Good

constant_value *= 2 # Calculate only once

for i in range(1000):
```

```
var result = constant_value
```

- **Use** range() **for Iterating through Arrays:** for i in range(array.size()): is generally more efficient than for item in array:, especially for large arrays.
- **Limit nested loops:** Nested loops increase complexity exponentially. Try to find alternate solutions if performance is critical.

4. Use Built-in Functions:

Godot's built-in functions (e.g., Vector2.distance_to(), lerp(), clamp()) are often optimized at a lower level (C++) and are generally faster than implementing the same logic in GDScript.

5. Avoid Excessive String Operations:

String concatenation and manipulation can be relatively slow. If you need to perform many string operations, consider using StringBuilder (if available in your Godot version) or other more efficient string manipulation techniques.

6. Object Pooling:

For objects that are frequently created and destroyed (e.g., bullets, particles), use object pooling. This involves creating a pool of objects at the start of the game and then reusing them instead of constantly creating and destroying new objects. This reduces memory allocation overhead.

Example Object Pooling:

GDScript

```
extends Node

export var bullet_scene : PackedScene

var bullet_pool = []

export var pool_size = 20

func _ready():

    for _i in range(pool_size):

        var bullet = bullet_scene.instance()

        bullet_pool.append(bullet)

        add_child(bullet)

        bullet.visible = false

func get_bullet():

    if bullet_pool.size() > 0:

        var bullet = bullet_pool.pop_front()

        bullet.visible = true

        return bullet

    else:

        print("Bullet pool empty!")

        return null

func return_bullet(bullet):
```

```
bullet.visible = false

bullet_pool.append(bullet)
```

---

7. Avoid Excessive Use of Signals:

While signals are great for decoupling, excessive use can lead to performance overhead, especially if you have many connections. Consider alternative approaches (like direct function calls or using groups) if performance is critical.

8. Use the Profiler:

Godot has a built-in profiler that can help you identify performance bottlenecks in your code. You can access it from the "Debugger" menu. The profiler shows you how much time is spent in different parts of your code, allowing you to focus your optimization efforts where they will have the greatest impact.

9. Consider Lower-Level Languages (GDNative/C++):

For extremely performance-critical sections of your game (e.g., complex physics simulations or AI algorithms), you might consider using C++ to write GDNative extensions. GDNative allows you to write code in C++ that can be loaded and used in your Godot projects. This can provide significant performance improvements.

10. Optimize Collision Shapes:

Use the simplest collision shapes possible. Avoid using complex polygon collision shapes if simpler shapes (like circles or rectangles) will suffice.

11. Batch Rendering (For 2D):

Godot automatically batches rendering of similar objects (e.g., sprites with the same texture). Make sure your sprites are using the same texture and material whenever possible to take advantage of batch rendering.

By following these tips, you can significantly improve the performance of your GDScript code and create smoother and more responsive games. Remember to use the profiler to identify specific bottlenecks in your project.

Conclusion

This comprehensive guide has covered a wide range of topics related to GDScript and game development in Godot. From the basics of GDScript syntax and data types to more advanced concepts like signals, scene management, UI creation, debugging, and optimization, you've gained a solid foundation for creating your own games.

Key Takeaways:

- **GDScript Fundamentals:** You've learned the basic syntax, data types, operators, control flow statements (if/else, for/while loops), functions, and classes in GDScript.
- **Object-Oriented Programming (OOP):** You understand the core principles of OOP, including inheritance, polymorphism, encapsulation, and abstraction, and how they apply to GDScript.
- **Godot's Scene Tree:** You're familiar with the hierarchical structure of the scene tree and how to access and manipulate nodes using GDScript.
- **Signals and Events:** You know how to use signals for communication between objects, creating custom signals, and connecting them to functions.
- **Input Handling:** You've learned how to handle keyboard, mouse, gamepad, and touch input using actions and the Input singleton.
- **Game Logic and Mechanics:** You understand how to implement basic game mechanics like movement and collisions using KinematicBody2D and Area2D.
- **Game State Management:** You know how to manage game state and data using variables, singletons (autoloads), and saving/loading data.

- **UI Creation:** You've learned how to create user interfaces using Control nodes, containers, and scripting UI behavior.
- **Debugging and Optimization:** You're familiar with the Godot debugger and have learned tips for optimizing GDScript performance.

Where to Go From Here:

- **Practice, Practice, Practice:** The best way to improve your skills is to work on projects. Start with small, simple games and gradually increase the complexity as you become more comfortable.
- **Explore the Godot Documentation:** The official Godot documentation is an excellent resource for learning more about specific nodes, classes, and functions.
- **Study Other People's Code:** Examining the code of open-source Godot projects can provide valuable insights and help you learn new techniques.
- **Join the Godot Community:** The Godot community is very active and supportive. You can find help, tutorials, and inspiration on the Godot forums, Discord server, and other online platforms.
- **Create Your Own Projects:** Don't be afraid to experiment and try new things. The most important thing is to have fun and keep learning!

By continuing to learn and practice, you'll be well on your way to becoming a proficient Godot game developer. This guide has provided you with a strong foundation, and the rest is up to you. Good luck, and have fun creating amazing games!

www.ingramcontent.com/pod-product-compliance
Lightning Source LLC
LaVergne TN
LVHW080117070326
832902LV00015B/2644